LIVERPOC

A Decade of Change and Cha   ...u rageuy

Tommy Allen

Acknowledgements

I would like to thank Bernie Doyle for his invaluable support and advice in producing this book and John Feegan for his painstaking proof-reading. I would also like to thank the staff at the Liverpool Record Office, William Brown Library for their courtesy and assistance with my research.

Text copyright © 2016 Tommy Allen

All Rights Reserved

Contents

Introduction 4

1. The Port and Shipping: A Great Leap Forward 8
2. Health and Welfare Campaigns and Campaigners 57
3. The Economic Divide: Poverty, Wealth, Leisure and Charity 88
4. Crime and Punishment 137
5. Black '47': Liverpool and the Great Irish Famine 179
6. Sectarian Town: Rebellious Town 198

Epilogue 215

Introduction

Liverpool has a history of transformative decades worthy of study, for example, the 1940s when the German Luftwaffe brought devastation and destruction which forced the city to undergo enormous change in the second half of the twentieth century. However, what emerges if the clock is turned back a further hundred years to the 1840s, is a decade of incredible change in terms of work, health, population, the geographical nature of the town and as a consequence of the change, the challenges faced and endured by the people of Liverpool.

Liverpool in 1841 was a relatively small town in size. Bounded by the fields of Kirkdale in the north, Everton and Edge Hill in the east and Toxteth in the south its official population was 286,487. The size of the population, relative to its geographical size, made Liverpool the most densely populated town in Britain in 1841. Although there was an increase in housing stock in the 1840s, the density worsened as Liverpool's population rose to an official 375,955. By comparison, consider the size of Liverpool in 2011 with a census population of 465,000.

Liverpool's development as one of the world's leading ports was the primary reason for population growth. Chapter one therefore opens with the rapid change to the port during the 1840s, when the number of docks doubled and several new shipping lines, such as Cunard, were established. In a grand ceremony, the town's most famous and iconic dock, the Albert, opened during the decade. Liverpool was both a merchandise and passenger port; it soon became the world's largest emigrant port, transporting people to all parts of the globe.

Although most passengers enjoyed trouble free journeys, there were problems for some travellers. One American, arriving and departing the port, had a particularly unhappy experience, which he methodically detailed. Much worse, disasters of all kinds struck some passenger ships resulting in massive loss of life.

Many of the poorer would-be emigrants arriving in Liverpool got no further than the town and added to the growth in population and, by association, the problem of the already overcrowding housing. The desperately poor quality insanitary housing conditions facilitated the spread of killer diseases such as cholera and typhus which wreaked havoc. Some local citizens responsible for tackling Liverpool's health and welfare problems, such as Doctor William Henry Duncan and William Rathbone, are the subjects of chapter two.

Chapter three examines the town's huge economic divide. The port's development brought great wealth to Liverpool's merchant and business classes many of whom spent lavishly on desired luxury goods and in their spare time on leisure activities such as theatre-going, concerts and horse racing at the newly opened Aintree racecourse; Liverpool was one of the first towns in the country to open a permanently based zoo, which proved enormously popular.

A town of great wealth, Liverpool though was also a place of great poverty and inequality and much of the populace could have only dreamt of spending their income on the luxuries of the wealthier classes. Tens of thousands, not all unemployed it should be added, lived in dire poverty in the overcrowded housing. The docks and their associated industries employed most workers, but for many, casualism (employment by chance) and its poverty inducing nature, was the order of the day. Meanwhile, beckoning for the desperate poor, was the reconstructed workhouse, opened in 1841 and administered by the Liverpool Parish.

There were a few wealthy individuals concerned about the consequences of poverty and several them did donate some of their considerable wealth to charity and charitable works; orphans, ex-female prisoners and pregnant married women were amongst those receiving assistance, although the help usually came with a religious element attached.

Poverty was undoubtedly a cause of crime (the subject of chapter four) and it was common for individuals to admit to committing offences to receive a prison sentence in order to simply eat (prison being preferable to the workhouse). Daily, dozens of relatively petty criminals, arrested by the recently formed Liverpool Police Force, appeared before the magistrates, whilst serious crimes such as murder, of which there was more than one notorious case, were dealt with at the quarterly assize courts.

Those found guilty of murder faced the death penalty, performed in public, usually before a hostile crowd, in the field outside Kirkdale Prison, one of two jails in Liverpool at the time. Young women who lost children during childbirth could too find themselves charged with infanticide, the murder of a child.

Chapter five examines the major cause of population increase in the 1840s. The arrival of tens of thousands of Irish migrants, fleeing the devastating Great Potato Famine which struck their country in 1845, increased the pressure and problems facing Liverpool. The authorities desperately sought solutions to the difficulties brought by the starving, distressed Irish, many of whom arrived carrying diseases such as typhus. Liverpool already held the unwanted, ignominious title of the *'unhealthiest town in the country'* before the arrival of the Irish refugees.

The final chapter analyses the issues of sectarianism, politics and rebellion. Liverpool was a town of sectarian division long before the Great Famine, as Catholics and Protestants engaged in violent clashes during the first three decades of the nineteenth century. The 1840s was no exception to this problem. As Ireland was part of the UK in the nineteenth century, many rebellious Irishmen and women, including hundreds living in Liverpool, campaigned for independence, causing great consternation among the British establishment.

Simultaneously, and causing equal concern, was the Chartist campaign for greater parliamentary rights and representation for the working class. The government, through overt and covert police methods, were determined to bring down the Irish rebels and Chartists.

* * * * *

The book, a non-academic piece of work, is aimed at a reader who holds a general interest in history and especially in the history of Liverpool. However, despite the lack of footnotes for example, the sources used are identified throughout the text.

1. The Port and Shipping: A Great Leap Forward

In the nineteenth century, after London, Liverpool rose to become the second port of the British Empire and one of the world's most important seaports. It is the River Mersey and the development of the docks for which the city of Liverpool owes its very existence. The link between the river and the city dates from its earliest recorded history when in 1207 King John, requiring a port from which to launch a planned invasion of Ireland, chose the then tiny village of Liverpool in which to establish a base.

Although growth was slow over the next few centuries, by the beginning of the eighteenth-century Liverpool's international importance was gaining momentum. Increasing trade with the Americas, involving for instance, sugar from the West Indies and tobacco from Virginia in the USA, boosted the economy and lead to further investment in the docks. The Americas trade relied heavily on the African slave trade; in 1700 parliament granted its approval to the involvement of Liverpool ships in the transatlantic trade, competing with existing slaving vessels from London and Bristol.

By the second half of the eighteenth century, Liverpool had overtaken its rivals to emerge as the world's largest slave trading port. Liverpool's population, increasing rapidly, provides an illustration of the town's development during this period rising from an estimated 7,000 in 1700 to over 77,000 in 1801.

The slave trade, viewed by many in the town as essential to the survival and development of the port, was, however about to be brought to an end. Many people in the UK were appalled by the trade in human beings and some, angry enough to act to bring about its abolition, established campaign groups to highlight the *'immoral and inhuman'* treatment of enslaved Africans.

As the eighteenth century turned in to the nineteenth, public, heated arguments for and against the trade's continuance were played out on the streets, in the press and in parliament. Both sides used parliamentary petitions to support their cases and one such, signed by Liverpool merchants, councillors and MPs, stressed that the town and port's future financial welfare and livelihood were in great danger, should the government introduce abolition. A 1798 petition implored the government:

> *'against the abolition of this source of wealth ...which so essentially concerns the welfare of the town and port of Liverpool in particular.'*

Despite the great profits brought by the slave trade, in 1807 the UK government voted for its abolition. The prophecies of doom, such as those espoused by the 1798 petitioners, proved to be entirely unfounded as the port went from strength to strength without reliance on the slave trade. Merchant trade with the Americas, and other parts of the world too, grew after abolition. The import and export of raw materials and finished goods expanded in the first decades of the nineteenth century and so in consequence did the port and the town. Liverpool was indeed on the rise.

However, in the nineteenth century, it was the 1840s which was to witness the most substantial expansion of the port when the number of docks in operation almost doubled. The Albert Dock, the port's most iconic, opened in the middle of the decade and its prolonged existence owes a great deal to the advancement in building technology. A consequence of several very destructive fires which destroyed warehouses and other workplaces, Liverpool Dock Trustees desperately required a solution to the devastation wreaked. They needed ideas and plans for the construction of buildings which could at least control and prevent devastation, as well as save lives. The Albert Dock's longevity is proof that the search for a solution was indeed successful.

When the new dock opened, Liverpool merchant ships were sharing the quay space with emigrant ships sailing in increasing numbers to different parts of the globe. The development, introduction and expansion of steamships, alongside the long-established sailing ships, dramatically reduced sailing times and made ocean-going travel more attractive. The USA, Canada and Australia in particular were desperate for emigrants to swell their populations and many hundreds of thousands of British and other Europeans were just as desperate to start new lives in those countries.

On the edge of Western Europe, Liverpool was in the perfect location to take advantage of the emigrant trade. Thus recently established shipping companies, such as the *Cunard Line,* made the port their home. The journey across the Atlantic was of course two-way and many Americans visited Britain and other European destinations via Liverpool. Passengers who enjoyed a pleasant journey were often complimentary about their experience, but, for some, the passage was not as satisfying as it was for their fellow travellers. Furthermore, ocean-going travel could be a dangerous affair and, for several reasons, there was always a risk of disaster at sea.

Liverpool's Greatest Dock Engineer

James Picton – the renowned Liverpool historian and architect described him as:

> *'A man of original genius, he guided with a despotic sway the construction of the mightiest works ever erected... he was rough in manner and occasionally rude, using expletives which the angel of mercy would not like to record.'*

The man described by Picton was a Yorkshireman, Jesse Hartley, who in 1824 was appointed as 'Civil Engineer and Superintendent of the Concerns of the Dock Estate of Liverpool.'

Born in Pontefract in 1780, Hartley, as a teenager, began working for his stonemason father. He went on to become an architect and bridge builder, travelling and working as far afield as London and Ireland before taking up his post in Liverpool. Over the next 36 years, until his retirement, he was responsible for the design of every new dock constructed or older dock altered on the ten mile stretch of the Mersey coastline. In the 1830s Clarence, Brunswick, Waterloo and Trafalgar docks were opened.

Under Hartley's stewardship, the largest growth in the extension of the dock system and warehousing occurred in the 1840s when eight new docks - Coburg (1840), Toxteth (1841), Albert (1846), Stanley (1848), Collingwood (1848), Nelson (1848), Bramley-Moore (1848) and Salisbury (1848) - opened during the decade. Hartley also designed other important buildings, some of which are still in use today, including the pumphouse at the Albert Dock and the six-sided Victoria clock tower at Salisbury Dock. Four other Hartley designed docks were added in the 1850s, Wellington, Huskisson, Wapping and Canada.

Picton described Hartley as despotic, a sentiment with which Nancy Ritchie-Noakes in her autobiography of the engineer *(Jesse Hartley, Dock Engineer to the Port of Liverpool, 1824-60)* would concur. She states that he wanted to do things to his design and that he was *'ruthless and meticulous'* in seeing his work carried out to the letter. There are stories of him visiting some of his designs under construction and, not liking what he saw, having workers dismissed.

The problems of older warehousing, says Ritchie-Noakes, meant Hartley was eager to incorporate new designs and new materials in future buildings. Pre-mid-nineteenth century warehouses were mostly constructed from wood and therefore destructive fires were a constant hazard and there were many in and around the docks before the 1840s. The problem of fires facing Hartley and his employers are illustrated by the following incidents.

Around 3.00 a.m. on Friday 23 September 1842, policeman Joseph Massey, patrolling Robert Street, close to the docks, spotted a fire developing in a warehouse. Failing to extinguish the flames, Massey called for assistance, but by the time the Liverpool Fire Police arrived the fire had rapidly spread to other warehouses including those in adjoining Formby Street. Many of the warehouses stored highly combustible substances including varnish, oil, turpentine and cotton: it was also a night of high winds; all in all, a very dangerous cocktail of ingredients.

Fire engines, 16 in total, eventually attended the spreading inferno, as thousands of onlookers gathered to watch the spectacle. It took over 24 hours for the fire police to bring the blaze under control, however, by then, 16 warehouses, five sheds, two cooperages, plus a couple of timber yards and stables had been destroyed, with the cost of damage estimated at around £500,000. Tragically, the fire also cost seven people their lives. All those who died, four warehouse workers and three fire policemen, Samuel Hodgson, Samuel Tuck and Joseph Bates, were not killed by fire or smoke but by collapsing buildings. The coroner's inquests returned verdicts of accidental deaths on the victims. Hodgson's inquest jury asked for their entitlement fee, a total of just over £1, to be donated to the fire policeman's father. On the day of his funeral, as the cortege made its way to his burial plot in St James' Cemetery, thousands of people lined the streets of Liverpool to pay their respects.

The enormous fire caused great consternation among the Liverpool populace. This was reflected in the local newspapers including the *Liverpool Journal* which on 16 October deplored the loss of life and damage saying the blazes were preventable. The newspaper claimed that warehouses:

> '...were often constructed too close to wooden sheds, steam engines, oil and paint shops and other reservoirs of accidents.'

The newspaper called for council and dock committees to regulate the building of warehousing and urged them both to prevent workmen smoking in warehouses.

As a consequence of the fire, Liverpool Fire Police were supplied with four new engines, but the most significant response was the introduction of a local act, *'The Better Protection of Property in the Borough of Liverpool from Fire'*, passed in 1843. The act gave the council powers to oversee fire safety measures in warehouses. Such buildings had to be registered and warehousemen in charge of the premises had the powers to stop and search people entering. Despite the best intentions of the new act, however, the nature and condition of numerous storage facilities and workplaces meant the threat of fires was ever present.

Mayor of Liverpool in 1832, Alderman Sir Thomas Brancker, from a long-established wealthy Liverpool family, owned a 4,000 square yards 'sugar house' (in modern parlance, a refinery), employing around 130 people in an eight-storey building located between Mathew Street and Harrington Street in the town centre. Sugar houses were extremely hot and dangerous places in which to work. Temperatures often reached over 100 degrees Fahrenheit and, as a consequence, many employees, including those at Brancker's factory, worked naked except for an apron to protect their modesty.

Around 8.15 a.m. on the morning of 28 December 1843, as most of the 65 men present were taking a breakfast rest, Brancker's sugar house caught fire. Reported in the *Liverpool Mail* the following day, the cause of the blaze appeared to be as a consequence of an explosion in a stove situated on a middle floor in the centre of the building. One of the employees, James Henry, opened the stove and in doing so '*was thrown backwards by the force of the explosion*' and the resultant fire spread rapidly. Those working on the floors below were able to escape quite quickly, but those on the upper floors were trapped by the smoke and flames.

The Fire Police were quickly on the scene raising ladders, which helped to rescue some of the workers on the Mathew Street side of the building, but they were not able to reach others on Harrington Street. Several workers took to sliding down red hot water pipes, whilst others jumped to safety on to lower roofs of adjoining buildings.

Serious injury resulted, but amazingly none escaping in this manner lost their lives. Tragically though, Robert Woods was killed, whilst Robert Roberts carried his housemate and workmate, Hugh Johns, from the fire. Roberts described Johns as being burnt *'from top to middle.'* Johns, who also shared his house on Mathew Street with a few workmates, died two days later in the Northern Hospital. Sustaining varying degrees of burns and a number with broken limbs, twenty employees were hospitalised in the Northern, fortunately, without further loss of life.

The *Journal* reported that Brancker, a Tory councillor for Castle Street Ward, arrived on the scene shortly after the fire started. He had temporarily stored some expensive paintings in the sugar house, which were in obvious danger of destruction. The paper however reported that Brancker's friend, Tory councillor, fellow businessman, builder, first president of the Conservative Tradesman's Association and eventual Lord Mayor in 1853, Samuel Holme, entered the blazing building to successfully rescue the paintings.

With little wind that morning, and passageways separating the sugar hose from neighbouring buildings, the Fire Police doused the flames and prevented the fire spreading. the firemen, though, could not prevent Brancker's sugar house from total destruction.

In 1841, to be called the Albert Dock in honour of queen Victoria's husband, the Dock Board Trustees assented to the construction of the largest warehouse system yet on the Mersey. The damaging fires regularly engulfing parts of the town, however, made Hartley more determined to construct warehouses that could at least prevent the spread of fire. Hartley aimed to show that his new design would prove that, should fire break out, it could at least be contained because of the application of fire proof materials, i.e. brick, stone and iron.

In 1843, to test his building materials, he constructed a model, 18 feet square and ten feet high, of warehouse arches at the Trentham Street Dockyard. He set fire to the model and the trustees observed as the materials proved fire resistant for over forty minutes, confirming the worthiness of Hartley's design. The demonstration was enough for the board to give Hartley the go-ahead to build the new dock.

To build the complex, Hartley used materials from many parts of the UK including huge grey Scottish granite stones, which were cut at the Dock Trustees' own quarry in Scotland. He also used red sandstone probably from a Runcorn quarry. Along much of the old shoreline of north Liverpool there was clay suitable for brick making. As new docks were built, the local clay excavated helped save money. Mortar was made to a careful recipe and this too proved very strong and water resistant. All around the Albert Dock complex, Hartley incorporated massive quayside columns to support the warehouses. These, still visible today, are made of hollow cast iron.

In 1845 the Albert Dock was opened to shipping and in July 1846 at a grand ceremony, though still not fully constructed, the dock was officially opened. On 30 July, sailing up the Mersey in the royal yacht Fairy in front of 4,000 specially selected onlookers, Prince Albert arrived to perform the opening ceremony.

The event was followed by a lunch for 600 invited guests at one of the dock warehouses. In the evening, the prince, who was staying at judges' lodgings in St. Anne Street, off Islington, travelled through the town passing thousands of cheering people to attend a five course

French banquet at the town hall. As darkness descended, an enormous firework display took place on the edge of the town. The next day, once more travelling along the town's main thoroughfares in front of cheering crowds, Prince Albert laid the foundation stone for the Sailors' Home in Canning Place.

The Liverpool docks impressed many visitors and arriving sailors. One such seaman, Herman Melville, the author of the famous seafaring novel Moby Dick, expressed his admiration in his semi-autobiographical novel *'Redburn: His First Journey'* (1849). He wrote:

> *'Vast pines of stone and granite-rimmed docks...The extent and solidity of these structures seemed equal to what I had read of the old pyramids of Egypt... In magnitude, cost and durability the docks of Liverpool even at the present day, surpass all others in the world.'*

Transatlantic Passenger Trade

By 1840, operating from Liverpool to America and Canada were several passenger lines using sailing ships. The ships provided accommodation for three classes, first, second and steerage, into which travellers were divided. First class cabin passengers fared as they might in a good hotel with a variety of food cooked and served to them, as well as having washing and toilet facilities provided. Though not as generous, those in the second-class cabins still had a plentiful supply of well-prepared food.

In steerage, the accommodation was very different. Passengers camped between decks, sleeping on narrow wooden bunks. They provided their own food and took their own utensils and bedding.

Washing and toilet facilities were minimal. There was almost no privacy and ventilation below deck was negligible.

In 1842 the government responding to the poor conditions passed the Passenger Act, a law that included regulations including the height between decks not to be less than 6 feet 2 inches; no deck for immigrants to be below the waterline; the compulsory carrying of lifeboats; a stock of medicines to be carried, though not a doctor; seven pounds of provisions were to be given out weekly and six pints of water daily per person. Although the regulations meant fewer passengers, conditions aboard were still harsh and companies would still pack in as many immigrants as they could.

Several attempts were made to establish regular lines in the 1830s, that is, a service with stated times of sailing from one year's end to another. The government, with the Royal Mail top of its agenda, was eager for companies to provide a regular and reliable transatlantic service. The government introduced mail service contracts and shipping companies fiercely vied with each other to win approval. The companies realised that steamships were the obvious future.

Having been used on American rivers for almost 40 years, steamships were not new. In 1819, the first Atlantic steamship, the New York built *Savannah* sailed from the Georgian port from which it was named, to Liverpool. Departing on 24 May, it reached Liverpool on 20 July after 27 days and 11 hours at sea. Despite the technological progress, steam shipping was slow to develop and not until 1837, with the establishment of the *British and American Steamship Navigation Company (BASNC)* did competition really begin. Its first paddle steamship, the *Sirius* sailed that year from Cork in southern Ireland to New York. In 1838 crossing the ocean in a time of 18 days and four hours, the vessel was quick enough to win the company the government contract to carry the Atlantic mail for the next two years.

The year before *Sirius'* maiden voyage, Isambard Kingdom Brunel, chief engineer of the *Great Western Railway Company,* set up the *Great Western Steamship Company*. Brunel designed his first ship, also named the *Great Western*, which set sail from Bristol to New York on 8 April 1838. With competition heating up, BASNC sought to expand its service and in 1840 it purchased a relatively quick paddle steamship, the *British Queen*. Also in that year, the company launched its first purpose built paddle steamer, the *President*, which was berthed in Liverpool.

In the meantime, Liverpool's own shipping line, the *Transatlantic Steamship Company of Liverpool*, had been both established and dissolved. The company owned just one ship named the *Liverpool*, which was well regarded by its users. In 1838, following the ship's passage from New York to Liverpool, travelling passengers presented its captain, Robert Fayrer, with an 18-carat gold snuff box. The inscription read:

> *'...from passengers as a token of their esteem and regard, and acknowledgment of his kind attention to their comforts during the passage.'*

The *Liverpool's* crossing was the first by a two-funnelled paddle steamer. The company though lost money on the voyage and, despite the praise received by Captain Fayrer, in 1839 the directors dissolved the company.

The pressure on shipping companies was enormous with rivals entering the market on a regular basis. In 1840 the established lines faced competition from what perhaps was to become Liverpool's most famous shipping company, the *Cunard Line*. Samuel Cunard, born in Halifax, Nova Scotia, Canada in November 1787, joined his father in the timber business and with interests that expanded into whaling, coal and iron as well as shipping; he had amassed a personal fortune by the 1830s. His shipping activities largely encompassed sailing ships, although he had some experience in early steam navigation as a shareholder in a wooden paddle steamer, the *Royal William* which in 1833 made a historic crossing of the Atlantic from Quebec to the Isle of Wight in just 17 days.

In 1839 Cunard submitted a bid to the British government to undertake a regular mail service across the Atlantic from Liverpool to the Canadian ports of Halifax and Québec and the US port of Boston. The bid was successful, and in the same year Cunard, with associates in Glasgow and Liverpool, established the *British and North American Royal Mail Steam Packet Company,* the predecessor of the *Cunard Line*. The first *Cunard* sailing ship crossed the Atlantic in May 1840 and in July its first steamer, *Britannia*, began the regular mail service, crossing from Liverpool to Halifax and then onto Boston in an impressive 14 days and 8 hours.

Speed of travel was vital for all companies, including *Cunard*, and one way to publicise the success of your ships was to win the coveted *Blue Riband*, awarded to the fastest ship to cross the Atlantic. From 1838 the *Great Western* held the honour, but *Cunard's* liner, the *Columbia*, surpassed Brunel's vessel travelling to Halifax in ten days, 14 hours.

Two years later the *Great Western* regained the honour which it then held for the next two. However, before the decade ended, three further *Cunard* liners *Cambria, America* and *Europa* all held the record. On its website today, the *Cunard Company* maintains that safety was the overriding concern of the owners in those early years. The company says Samuel Cunard gave specific instructions to his captains: *'Your ship is loaded, take her; speed is nothing, follow your own road, deliver her safe, and bring her back safe – safety is all that is required'*; evidently understandable giving the inherent dangers of the ocean-going travel.

The Unhappy Experiences of one American Passenger

The development of steamships led to a sizeable increase in the numbers of American businessmen, politicians, academics, entertainers and general tourists, arriving in the UK via Liverpool.

For some of these passengers, though, it was not the safety of the ships that concerned them, but the attitudes of some of their fellow passengers. One such traveller was American anti-slavery campaigner Frederick Douglass, who arrived in Liverpool aboard the Cunard owned *Cambria* on 28 August 1845. Douglass had endured a hostile journey and news of his experience caused consternation amongst many people in the UK. He arrived in Liverpool to embark on a 19-month tour of much of the UK spreading the anti-slavery message. The events leading up to his return journey aboard the same vessel was arguably more controversial than the incidence he experienced on his initial journey.

The son of a female slave and an unknown white man, Frederick Bailey (Douglass' birth name) was born in February 1818 in the US state of Maryland. While growing up on a slave plantation, he witnessed the degradations of slavery, for instance seeing first hand brutal whippings and beatings. At the age of eight he was sent to Baltimore to live with a ship's carpenter, Hugh Auld. It was there he learned to read and write and first encountered the campaign for abolition of slavery.

Frederick enjoyed seven relatively comfortable years in Baltimore before being sent back to the plantation upon which he was raised, where he was hired out to a farm run by a 'slave breaker' named Edward Covey. Here he was whipped daily and barely fed. He wrote later in his autobiography that he was *'broken in body, soul, and spirit.'* These events were to propel him to become an activist against slavery and, if the chance arose, he resolved that he would escape from it.

In 1838 Frederick was back living and working in a Baltimore shipyard and here he met his future wife, 25-year-old Anna Murray, a free black woman. In September of that year, with the encouragement of Anna, he took the decision to flee to New York and began his attempt to escape slavery. The couple married there and a few weeks later they moved to New Bedford, Massachusetts, where Frederick and Anna adopted the new surname, Douglass.

An avid reader, Douglass continued to educate himself. In New Bedford, he attended slave abolitionists' meetings where he met the prominent abolitionist William Garrison. He became a regular lecturer and author and in 1845 he published his first autobiography, *Narrative of the Life of Frederick Douglass, an American Slave*. The book's publication made him a target, as he was still regarded as a runaway slave, having never been officially freed from or bought out of slavery. Garrison and other supporters encouraged him to remove himself from the USA and publicise his book on the iniquities of slavery by embarking on a tour of the UK.

Arriving in Boston on 16 August 1845, Douglass boarded the *Cunard* owned Liverpool bound ship the *Cambria,* under the command of Captain Charles Judkins. He had a first-class ticket but never saw the inside of his cabin, being relegated to steerage because his colour. There was a wide array of passengers on board including doctors, lawyers, soldiers and sailors, Catholic bishops, Protestant ministers and Quakers, government officials from Canada, a diplomat from Spain and slaveholders from Cuba and Georgia.

Moving around the ship with his white anti-slavery companions, Douglass, under advice, stayed clear of the main saloon-deck until the day before the *Cambria* was due to dock. Captain Judkins invited Douglass to address an audience after informing him that some of the ship's passengers were keen to hear his views on slavery and slave laws.

What happened next became something of a sensation amongst parts of the British public. His story of that day's events spread after his arrival in Liverpool. In December on a tour of Ireland, Douglass informed an audience in Belfast of his experience that day. The Belfast based newspaper, the *Banner of Ulster* as well as other Irish papers, published Douglass' story on 9 December. The paper wrote:

> *'When he went forward to the saloon-deck, to address his audience, there was one group which was resolved that he should not speak. He found them cursing and swearing towards him; but the Captain introduced him to the passengers.*
>
> *He proceeded to address them, but he had uttered hardly five words, when one of the slaveholders stepped up to him, shook his stick in his face, and said it was a lie. Mr. Douglass then said he would give them a few facts and then read a list of laws from the slaveholders' code of regulations with regard to the slave, in which*

the most cruel and barbarous punishments, such as lashings on the back, the cropping of ears and other revolting disfigurements, were awarded for the most minor 'crimes', and even frequently when no crime whatever had been committed.

The reading of these before the audience caused the slaveholders, on the occasion, to writhe in utter agony. One of them said that he would be one of a number to throw Douglass overboard. There happened to be on board an Irishman who hinted that two might possibly play at that game. That had a very good and salutary effect upon the young man.

> *Threats were urged by the slaveholders against Mr. Douglass but the Captain said that he must have a respectful hearing and he would see that order was maintained. Some of them were so outrageous in their conduct, that the Captain at last said, he would put them in irons — the irons were brought forward, and the slaveholders, who had been so brave and courageous, sneaked away to different parts of the ship.'*

Following his arrival in Liverpool, Douglass embarked on his 19-month tour of all major towns and cities in the UK, addressing audiences which on occasion amounted to thousands. He returned to Liverpool on 23 October 1846 to deliver a speech to an anti-slavery audience of 2,500 at the *Concert Hall*, Lord Nelson Street. He expressed how good it felt to be free and not to have a slave master forever threatening him. In a later autobiography (*My Bondage My Freedom*: 1855) he wrote of his reception in Liverpool:

'*Instead of meeting the curled lip of scorn and seeing the face of hatred all was blandness and kindness. I looked around for expressions of insult... there was not one look of scorn or enmity.*'

With his tour ending in London, in March 1847, Douglass arrived at the capital's *Cunard* office to purchase a return ticket for a private cabin aboard the *Cambria*, travelling from Liverpool to Boston. In April, Douglass took up lodgings in Liverpool. On the 3rd however, the day before he was set to sail and when passengers were expected to deposit their baggage aboard ship, Douglass was refused entry to his cabin. That evening, returning to his accommodation at *Brown's Temperance Hotel* in Clayton Square, Douglass wrote of his experience in a letter to the *London Times*, presenting his version of recent events:

> *'On 4th of March last I called upon Mr. Foord, the London agent of the Cunard line of steamers, for securing a passage (from Liverpool) on board the steam-ship Cambria to Boston, United States. I received from him in return a ticket entitling me to berth number 72 at the same time asking him if my colour would prove any barrier to my enjoying all the rights and privileges enjoyed by other passengers. He said 'No.'*
>
> *I went on board the Cambria with my luggage, and on inquiring for my berth, found, to my surprise that it had been given to another passenger, and was told that the agent in London had acted without authority in selling me the ticket. I expressed my surprise and disappointment to the captain, and inquired what I had better do in the matter. He suggested my accompanying him to the office of the agent in Water-street, Liverpool, for ascertaining what could be done.*
>
> *On stating the fact of my having purchased the ticket of the London agent, Mr. McIver (the Liverpool agent) answered that the London agent, in selling me the ticket, had acted without authority,*

> and that I should not go on board the ship unless I agreed to take my meals alone, not to mix with the saloon company, and to give up the berth for which I had paid. Anxious to return to the United States, I have felt it due to my own rights as a man, as well as to the honour and dignity of the British public, to lay these facts before them, sincerely believing that the British public will pronounce a just verdict on such proceedings. I have travelled in this country 19 months, and have always enjoyed equal rights and privileges with other passengers.'

McIver, a brother of David one of the founders of the *Cunard Line*, was placed under further pressure, On 6 April a letter from William Shortt appeared in the *Liverpool Mercury*. Shortt had accompanied Douglass to the *Cunard* office, He wrote:

> 'McIver told him (Douglass) that Foord had no right to sell him the ticket and that he should eat alone on the ship... As he wanted to go home as soon as possible, Douglass acceded to the conditions.'

In the same edition, the *Mercury*, accepting Shortt's version, was clearly angered by the treatment meted out to Douglass and claimed that it was:

> 'Disgraceful that a human being should be wronged, insulted and tabooed on board a vessel in the service of Great Britain for no other reason than the colour of his skin.'

McIver though, just as clearly upset at the developing narrative, disputed Douglass' version in letters to the *Times* and the *Mercury* on 12 April. He wrote that when the men met in his Water Street office, 'Douglass had already agreed to be excluded from his accommodation' aboard ship and that the American had come to this conclusion owing to his experience on his original journey to Liverpool. McIver claimed he would not have prevented any passenger, regardless of colour, from being excluded from his cabin.

The following day a letter purporting to be from Charles M. Burrop, Manager of Cunard Liners Virginia, USA appeared in the *Times*. In it he stated that Douglass was rightly excluded from his berth because of an:

> *'...absolute disgust on the part of a great many white men and particularly white women to come into close contact with blackamores.'*

This correspondence forced Samuel Cunard to get involved in an attempt to conclude the unsavoury episode and to try to clarify the company's position. Again, writing to the *Times* he declared the Burrop letter a hoax, saying no such person was employed by Cunard. He concluded:

> *'No one can regret more than I do the unpleasant circumstances regards Mr Douglass passage; but I can assure you that nothing of the kind will take place in the steam ships with which I am connected.'*

Douglass however never accepted McIver's version of events of his experience. In a later letter to William Garrison he wrote that McIver behaved with *'the harshness of an American slaveholder.'* During his tour of the UK Douglass became legally free, as British supporters raised funds to buy his freedom from his American owner Hugh Auld.

Alternative Experiences of American Passengers

In 1849 a fellow African-American anti-slavery campaigner, William Wells Brown, sailed from Boston to Liverpool and underwent a totally different experience to that of Frederick Douglass, one that must have pleased Samuel Cunard. A prominent lecturer, novelist, playwright, and historian, Wells Brown was born into slavery in Kentucky in 1814. At the age of 20 he escaped to Ohio. He eventually settled in Boston, where he worked for the abolitionist cause and became a writer. In 1849 he followed in the footsteps of Douglass crossing the Atlantic aboard the Cunard owned steamship *Canada*. The ship was under the command of Charles Judkins, former captain of the *Cambria* upon which Douglass sailed in 1847.

Unlike Douglass, Wells Brown travelled as a cabin passenger and according to his 1852 memoir, *Three Years in Europe; or, Places I Have Seen and People I Have Met*, the journey appears to have been an enjoyable experience. He did write that he had encountered *'some prejudice'* aboard the *Canada*, but did not go into detail about the form it took or from where it came. Of the first seven days of the journey he wrote of a *'pleasant passage.'* He added:

> 'The last night on board was the most pleasant that we had experienced... The next morning I was up before the sun, and found that we were within a few miles of Liverpool... The passage had only been nine days and twenty-two hours, the quickest on record at that time.'

Upon reaching shore Wells Brown was *'soon comfortably installed at Brown's Temperance Hotel, Clayton Square'*, the same accommodation as Douglass. He concluded:

> 'No person of my complexion can visit this country without being struck with the marked difference between the English and the Americans. The prejudice which I have experienced vanished as soon as I set foot on the soil of Britain. No sooner was I on British soil, then I was recognised as a man, and an equal... Such is the difference, and such is the change that is brought about by a trip of nine days in an Atlantic steam.'

Samuel Cunard, if he ever did hear, must have been pleased with the words of Wells Brown, as they were similar to the promises he made to passengers in his 1848 *Times*' letter.

Herman Melville in his semi-autobiographical novel *Redburn*, compared the experience of his fellow black crew members in Liverpool with their experiences in his home town, New York. He wrote that he rarely saw a black face during his six week stay in the town, but, like Douglass, he was praiseworthy of the town when it came to his observations of the experiences of his fellow black crewmen. He wrote:

> 'In Liverpool, indeed the negro steps with a prouder pace, and lifts his head like a man; for here, no such exaggerated feeling exists in respect to him, as in America. Three or four times, I encountered our black steward, dressed very handsomely, and walking arm in arm with a good-looking English woman. In New York, such a couple would have been mobbed in three minutes; and the steward would have been lucky to escape with whole limbs. Owing to the friendly reception extended to them, the black cooks and stewards of American ships are very much attached to the place and like to make voyages to it.'

Liverpool may have been a more racially tolerant town than most US towns and cities, however, it may not have been as harmonious as Melville, Douglass and Wells Brown assumed it to be, particularly with respect to relationships between black men and white women. On 20 July 1844, reporting on events at the Magistrates Court, the *Liverpool Mercury* wrote of two Americans, a white female stewardess, Arabella Down, and a black male steward, William Blake, of the US steamship *Washington Irving*, walking arm in arm on Robert Street. There they were approached by a man who shouted racial abuse at Blake and then struck Arabella Down knocking her to the ground.

The un-named defendant was severely reprimanded by Chief Magistrate Edward Rushton and fined £5. On leaving the court, however, Down was again assaulted by what the newspaper described as *'a group of friends of the prisoner.'* The police were called and Rushton appealed to Head Constable Dowling to apprehend the assailants. There were no reports as to whether Dowling was successful in executing the order.

The *Mercury* reported on another racially motivated assault on 19 March 1847. Headlined *'An Enemy of the Black Race,'* the paper informed readers of the case of John Waters of Vauxhall who was charged with assaulting John Fishburne. The victim informed the court that he had left church on a Sunday evening in the company of a female friend when Waters made remarks about the difference in colour between the couple. Waters then struck Fishburne knocking him to the ground and threatened the woman. Only for the intervention of passers-by, the court heard, was further violence prevented. The interveners held Waters until his arrest.

In court, Waters admitted using the remarks attributed to him but denied using violence. Magistrate Rushton, nevertheless, chose to accept the evidence of Fishburne telling Waters *'I will teach you to respect all persons without reference to the colour of their skin.'* He found Waters guilty and fined him £5 or alternatively, should he default in paying the fine, two weeks' imprisonment.

Frederick Douglass and William Wells Brown both lived on through the American Civil War and, in 1865, witnessed the abolition of American slavery. Anna Douglass died in 1882; Wells Brown in 1884 and Frederick Douglass in February 1895. Earlier this century historical plaques were installed on buildings in Cork and Waterford in Ireland and also in London to commemorate Douglass' visit. There is too a mural dedicated to Douglass on the Falls Road in Belfast.

The Dangers of Ocean-going Travel

In the 1840s travelling the world's oceans could be a dangerous, treacherous affair. Travelling first class, though preferable to other accommodation, did not make the crossing any less perilous. Charles Dickens, with his wife Catherine and her maid Anne Brown, crossed from Liverpool to Boston on the *Cunard* owned *Britannia* during a January 1842 storm. He recounted their Atlantic journey in his travelogue, *American Notes for General Circulation* (1842):

> *'But what the agitation of a steam-vessel is, on a bad winter's night in the wild Atlantic, it is impossible for the most vivid imagination to conceive. To say that she is flung down on her sides in the waves, with the waves dipping into them, and that, springing up again, she rolls over on the other side, until a heavy sea strikes her with the noise of a hundred great guns,*

and hurls her back—that she stops, staggers, and shivers, as though stunned, and then, with a violent throbbing of her heart, darts onward like a monster goaded into madness to be beaten down, and battered, and crushed, and leaped on by the angry sea.'

The steamship experience certainly left a negative impression on Dickens as he returned to Liverpool six months later aboard a sailing ship. If Atlantic steamship travel was a dreadful experience for Dickens travelling first class, it was very much worse for most passengers, especially for those who travelled cheaply in steerage.

Storms, though commonplace, were not the only danger. Hygiene was poor at the best of times and worse in bad weather. The cry of *'batten down the hatches'* meant passengers in steerage were confined to their accommodation without ventilation or light. The use of candles or oil lanterns was restricted and sometimes forbidden. Cramped conditions with timber, straw mattresses, rope, flammable liquids such as alcohol and tar caulking, meant a fire could spread with terrifying speed. A disaster at sea or shipwreck on the coast left little hope for rescue, most passengers would not have been able to swim; they had little reason to learn. Moreover, there were rarely enough life-boats for the number of passengers on board.

Calm weather or a loss of direction, could represent a risk too, slowing down ships and putting a strain on food and water supplies. For example, the *Liverpool Journal* of 22 Jan 1842, reported on the aftermath of the journey of the *Normandie* from Liverpool to New York the previous year. The ship sailed from Liverpool on 21 October for an expectant passage across the Atlantic of around six weeks. The journey though lasted nine weeks and the 199 passengers, who were expected to supply their own food, were threatened with starvation.

The *Normandie's* captain, James Spalding, rationed what remained of the crew's supply, but this was barely enough for the number of passengers aboard.

There is no evidence of anyone dying of starvation on the passage, but the reason behind the press interest was a subsequent New York coroner's inquest. The coroner heard that within two days of arrival in the port, ten-year-old Jane Pringle, who travelled with her parents and four siblings, had died. After hearing evidence from those involved, he returned a verdict of *'death due to starvation.'*

In addition to these hazards, by the mid 1840s the effects of the Great Irish Potato Famine heightened the danger of sea-going travel. The tens of thousands fleeing the ravages of crop failure were not only suffering from starvation, but also the consequences of highly infectious diseases such as typhus and cholera. Thus, many passengers boarding transatlantic immigrant ships spread infections to their fellow travellers.

Shipping disasters were a regular occurrence. The Liverpool press carried weekly reports of shipwrecks from all over the world. At the same time, they also carried dozens of adverts for emigrant ships travelling the globe. People were aware of the dangers but, notwithstanding, tens of thousands of them boarded Liverpool ships and were prepared to face the dangers of travelling the oceans in the hope of making a new life in America, Canada and Australia.

Steamship *President*

In the 1840s a passage across the Atlantic from Liverpool to New York of eleven to twelve days aboard a steamship was considered very acceptable. On Saturday 1 August 1840, the British and American Steamship Navigation Company's purpose built paddle steamer the *President* sailed from Liverpool to New York with 30 passengers aboard eager to cross in a similar time.

The company appointed the highly-regarded Captain Fayrer to command the vessel following the closure of the Transatlantic Steamship Company. The ship reached its destination on 17 August, a crossing of 16 days, which the company deemed highly unsatisfactory. Embarrassingly too for the company, the *President* was overtaken on her maiden voyage by the Cunard owned steamer *Acadia,* this even though *Acadia* had left Liverpool three days later than its rival.

Fayrer was held responsible for the slow passage and, on return to Liverpool, was dismissed and replaced by the captain of the *British Queen*, Richard Roberts. On 10 February 1841, with an upgrade of the ship's paddles, *President* again left Liverpool for New York. Regardless of the change in command and the technological improvement, *President*'s time was even slower than the previous year; the ship arrived on 2 March, a crossing of 20 days.

Because of *President*'s lack of speed its turnaround time was much shorter than usual. Captain Roberts did not want to remain in New York longer than scheduled. *President*, therefore, with a total of 136 passengers and crew, began its return journey to Liverpool on 11 March. Among its passengers was Tyrone Power, grandfather of the renowned mid 20th century actor of the same name. Captain Roberts was hoping to be in Liverpool before the end of the month. *President* had failed to dock in Liverpool by the end of March and there was no news of its imminent arrival. Concern and rumour of its whereabouts spread throughout the town. During early April, local newspapers were trying to allay the fears of the families and friends of the ship's crew and passengers by suggesting, for example, that *President* had, more than likely, contracted some engineering problems and the captain may have sailed to some other nearby port to resolve them.

By mid-April however, this seemed unlikely and on the 17th the Liverpool *Mail* speculated that the ship had crossed the Atlantic and berthed at the Portuguese island of Madeira. A week later the paper was showing its exasperation of what it termed *'various absurd and contradictory rumours that the ship was in Bermuda, Bordeaux or stuck in ice near Newfoundland.'*

On the 24th the paper's exasperation had turned to anger stating that, *'rumours are now not just annoying but disgusting, particularly those that had suggested that the ship had sunk.'* The paper appreciated that the ship may have suffered this fate, but until evidence emerged, rumour of such was cruel. It added that it had come across a ridiculous report in a Dublin newspaper suggesting that the *President* had arrived in Newfoundland. The report, the *Mail* quoted, came from it said:

> *'The editor who had heard from a gentleman, who had heard from Sir Philip Crompton, who had heard from a gentleman on a Kingstown train, that he had heard from a mate who had belonged to a ship called the Urgent, that he had heard from a Liverpool captain who had towed the President to Newfoundland.'*

As April turned to May newspaper reports on the *President* diminished. It became widely accepted that the ship had almost certainly been lost at sea. The following month the *Mail* carried a story that a ship's captain, returning to Bristol on 8 June from a long period at sea, reported that in mid-March he and his crew had spotted a lot of wreckage around the time and the location which coincided with the beginning of the *President*'s journey.

A week or so later news arrived of a New York inquiry into the *President*'s disappearance. Chaired by the British consul, the most compelling evidence came from Captain Lockman of a New York pilot boat, the *Orpheus*. He told the inquiry that a storm began raging in the north Atlantic on 13 March and that when he last saw the *President*:

> *'It was rising on the top of a tremendous sea; it appeared to be pitching heavily and labouring tremendously. The waves were as high as a four or five storey house.'*

Lockman added that the ship would have been shipping water heavily and fast. *'It would have been helpless,'* he concluded. Without doubt the *President* and all on board had been lost at sea.

Was the ship seaworthy? Did the quick turnaround affect the ship's performance? Did the need for speed ultimately lead to the deaths of 136 people? These questions cannot be conclusively answered with any degree of certainty. Whatever the conclusions, there was one absolute consequence of the disaster, the dissolution of the *British and American Steamship Navigation Company*.

The *Cataraqui*

In the spring of 1845 Solomon Brown, a 30-year-old labourer from Bedfordshire, was along with his family, preparing to travel to Liverpool. The family had made the life changing decision to emigrate to Australia. Many similar families across the country had been persuaded to do the same by adverts such as the one below which appeared in the *Worcestershire Chronicle* on 24 March (the local agents were listed.

NEW SOUTH WALES

A first-class ship will be despatched from Liverpool on 15th April 1845 and is the last under the present Bounty Contract. Agricultural labourers, shepherds, farm servants, bricklayers, blacksmiths, carpenters, stonemasons, wheelwrights, female domestics and farm servants may obtain a free passage from Liverpool to New South Wales where all persons connected with farming operations or stock are urgently required.

Apply to William Smith, 6 Exchange Buildings Liverpool or his local agents.

Australia was a relatively new, vast British colony desperate to attract young workers. In 1837 the British government's Colonial and Emigration Office had initiated the *'Bounty Contract'*, a system whereby emigrants from Britain had their transport paid by an Australian state government, in this case New South Wales, with the promise of guaranteed employment upon arrival.

A typical bounty, shared between the ship owners and agents, was about £30 for an adult and £5 for a child. The contract, however, had now ended and the Brown family was to travel on the last ship, the *Cataraqui*, to sail under the system. Since its inception more than

42,000 people had taken the opportunity to emigrate to Australia through the bounty contract.

As suggested in the advert, Australia was keen to attract young rural families such as the Browns. Most of these families were struggling to find regular work in the UK and many were therefore living in desperate poverty at the time of their departure. The great majority of *Cataraqui*'s emigrant families were forced to use the poor law to feed themselves.

An indication of their financial plight is evident in a report from the Browns' local newspaper the *Bedfordshire Mercury* of Saturday 19 April. Under the headline *'Pauper Emigration'* the paper stated that 33 people from six families (more than likely including the Browns) left Bedford for Liverpool on Monday 14 April to embark with free passages on their journey to Port Philip Bay, (Melbourne Australia). The report added:

> *'We understand that these poor families were well provided with warm clothes and other necessities at the expense of their local parishes and upon reaching their destinations they will be provided with employment.'*

The report concluded by claiming the families were likely to be better off in Australia than in Bedfordshire.

In Liverpool, the Bedfordshire families were joined by 60 others from counties such as Yorkshire, Nottinghamshire, Oxfordshire and Staffordshire. Their ship, the *Cataraqui*, was built in Quebec in 1840 and was owned by William Smith of Liverpool. The vessel, commanded by Dublin born, Liverpool resident and married father of two, Captain Christopher Findlay, was to be the first of the ship's captain. Also, undertaking his initial passage in a new post, was first mate Thomas Guthrie.

Under instruction, on the day they left Bedford, Solomon Brown, his wife Hanna aged 40 (the oldest female passenger), and their four children, Ellen 14, Phoebe 8, Elizabeth 5 and Ruth 9 months, deposited their baggage aboard the *Cataraqui*. At departure time, there were 369 passengers on board. There were 41 members of the crew most who were from Liverpool. Though originally booked to sail on 15 April, departure was delayed and *Cataraqui* did not set sail until the 20th of the month. The expected journey time was about fourteen weeks.

During a storm on 4 July, one able seaman, Robert Harvey, tragically lost his life when he was washed overboard. On 4 August, after one hundred days at sea and a day from its destination, the *Cataraqui* reached the southern coast of Australia. Sadly, six children had died on the journey although five were born. The ship had now entered the Bass Strait, a stretch of water which separates the coast of the southern state of Victoria on mainland Australia from the island of Tasmania. *Cataraqui* was though sailing into the teeth of a violent storm reaching its peak.

Off the north-western tip of Tasmania is King Island. *Cataraqui* was close to the island as the storm raged. Tasmanian newspaper *Launceston Examiner* of 17 September reported the subsequent events:

> *'Around 4 a.m. the Cataraqui crashed without warning on the jagged rocks about 150 yards offshore of King Island. Immediately after striking there was four feet of water in the hold, and despite the ladders leading below decks being knocked away, the crew managed to get most of the*

emigrants on deck. It proved of little use as huge seas swept the decks and washed scores overboard, to be battered to death on the rocks by the surf. At about 5 a.m. the ship rolled onto her beam ends, and more were thrown into the raging waters. The masts were cut away to ease her, but being full of water she did not respond.

Daylight found some 200 survivors still clinging to the wreck. At about 10 a.m. the last remaining boat was launched, but immediately capsized, drowning its five or six occupants.

Sometime afterwards the hull broke away and the stern began to collapse, throwing perhaps 70 to 100 into the water leaving about 70 survivors crowded onto the forecastle. Captain Finlay tried to swim ashore, but was forced back by the currents.

Finally, it was decided that the only chance of survival was to try to swim ashore on floating wreckage. First mate Thomas Guthrie crawled along a sail and was washed out. He reached shore clinging to two planks. Here he found an emigrant who had earlier come ashore, clinging to a piece of wreckage, and a seaman who had got ashore earlier in the morning. The forecastle broke up soon afterwards, throwing the handful of remaining survivors into the water, and of them six crewmen managed to get ashore safely. They were the last to reach shore alive.'

Along with Guthrie, the surviving crew members were able seamen William Jones, Francis Millen and John Roberts; ordinary seamen John Simpson, John Robertson and Peter Johnson; the last crewman to reach the safety of King Island was a teenage apprentice, William Blackstock. Had the crew taken the decision to save their own lives?

The sole surviving emigrant was Solomon Brown, who had witnessed the tragic deaths of his wife and four young children.

There were no long-term inhabitants living on the island, but Solomon and the eight crew members were lucky in that there was a party of seal hunters working and living there who were able to feed and shelter them. There was one other man also on the island, David Howie, known as the 'Constable of the Straits. Howie had been forced ashore the day before by the severity of the storm. The hunters were due to be picked up by ship. This finally arrived on 7 September and took them and the survivors to the safety of Tasmania.

On arrival, they told their stories of the disaster. The newspaper report above is taken from a statement given by first mate Guthrie, which soon travelled the world. He went on to say how during the days following the disaster the bodies of those drowned began to wash ashore. The survivors, Howie and the hunters began to bury the dead. There is no record, but it is more that probable than Solomon Brown was involved in the harrowing interment of the bodies of his wife and four children. When the enormous task was completed a total of 342 bodies had been buried in five mass graves, and several smaller ones.

Questioning the causes of the disaster the following year, a British Colonial and Emigration Office Enquiry Board, concluded that the ship was almost certainly off course and had sailed dangerously close to the reefs surrounding King Island. Among the board's primary concerns were the experience and the capabilities of Captain Finlay and first mate Guthrie.

The board invited *Cataraqui's* owner, William Smith, to respond. On 6 February 1846, in a letter of reply, he stated:

'We are informed that the reef of rocks on which she struck is a most fearful one, rendering it impossible for any vessel which unhappily was driven on them to escape destruction in a gale of wind. Captain Finlay was a well-educated, steady, experienced person, who was strongly recommended to us by his former employers, Brooke and Wilson of this town. Both the first and second mates were also steady, experienced men, fully qualified for the duties they undertook.'

The Colonial Office ultimately blamed the lack of safety precautions on King Island, namely the lack of a lighthouse. Even if Finlay was off course a warning signal would have alerted him of forthcoming dangers and he may have steered to safety.

The British government took the decision to prohibit emigrant vessels sailing through the Bass Strait until a lighthouse was constructed on the island. This decision had a dramatic negative effect on the Australian immigrant programme. The Australian colonial government almost immediately ordered the building of a lighthouse, which was eventually in use by 1848. Thereafter the emigrant trade to Australia began to revive.

Solomon Brown soon left Tasmania to take up residence in Melbourne. However, in the 1850s he moved to the town of Ballarat some 65 miles north west of Melbourne. In 1851 gold was discovered close to Ballarat and the town grew to become the central location in the subsequent Australian gold rush. Solomon went on to remarry an Australian woman, Ann Reid, who was 20 years his junior. In 1861 Ann gave birth to a child, Frances Ellen. Solomon lived out the remainder of his life in Ballarat. He died there in 1874.

The *Ocean Monarch*

Around 12 noon on Thursday 24 August 1848, about 25 miles from Liverpool, able seaman Frederick Jerome was attending to his duties aboard a New York ship, the *New World*. Jerome, born in Portsmouth, was at the time a married father of two living in New York. His ship, sailing from Liverpool to New York, was close to the Great Ormshead, off the North Wales coast.

Sailing nearby and returning to its home port of Liverpool was the *Queen of the Ocean*, a yacht owned by Liverpool merchant and Commodore of the Royal Mersey Yacht Club, Thomas Littledale. He and his fellow passengers had been taking part in the Beaumaris Regatta. Jerome, Littledale and others aboard their vessels would have observed another ship, the *Ocean Monarch,* about five or six miles away near Abergele Bay, pursuing its course to the Atlantic. The *Ocean Monarch* though was in serious trouble having hoisted a flag of distress.

Sailing under Captain James Murdoch the *Ocean Monarch*, a three masted emigration sailing ship, left Liverpool on that morning to travel to Boston in the United States. Aboard were 354 passengers, 322 in steerage with 32 in first and second class cabins. Also, aboard were 42 members of the crew. The ship, launched in July 1847 and registered in Boston, had undertaken a couple of trips between that port and Liverpool. The reason for the flag of distress was obvious to Littledale and the other observers. They saw flames emanating from the stern of *Ocean Monarch*. Aware that the ship was clearly in difficulty Littledale sailed towards the vessel with the purpose of rendering what assistance he could.

On nearing the vessel, a dreadful scene presented itself to Littledale. The flames had taken a strong hold and were quickly spreading from the stern to the rest of the ship. Passengers were crammed to the fore of the vessel and many in danger had taken to jumping overboard, tragically drowning in the process. Littledale upon arrival at the scene did, though, manage to pick up 32 survivors from the sea.

Apart from *New World,* there were other vessels nearby and they too came to *Ocean Monarch*'s assistance. Among them was a Brazilian steam frigate, *Affonso*, on a leisure cruise. With a very wealthy passenger list, *Affonso* included a member of the French royal family, Prince de Joinville.

The ship was commanded by Captain JM Lisboa; also in attendance was a paddle steamer, Prince of Wales, en route from Dublin to Liverpool. Lisboa lowered four rescue boats from his vessel and was also able to attach a rope from the *Affonso* to the *Ocean Monarch* enabling many passengers to scramble aboard his rescue ship. *Affonso* ultimately managed to rescue 156 passengers and crew.

Jerome's ship was the last to arrive on the scene when there were only about twelve passengers, all women and children, left aboard. They appeared too terrified to either use the rope or jump into the sea to be rescued. Jerome stripped naked and swam across to the burning vessel where he climbed aboard. There he tied a rope to each of the remaining passengers and lowered them down onto *Affonso* and to safety. Jerome was the last person to leave the ship.

The Liverpool *Mercury*, wrote of Jerome's bravery:

> *'His efforts were incredibly great: at the very least he preserved ten persons from destruction. His gallantry was conspicuous. The Prince de Joinville noticed him, and when he came on board, after his labours, called him on deck, shook hands warmly with him, complemented him eagerly, and in a manor, most princely presented him with a handful of gold coins.'*

Jerome went on to receive much praise from for his heroic deeds and other monetary rewards.

The *Ocean Monarch* eventually sank at 1.30. Although the rescue ships and boats were able to save the lives of 218 passengers and crew 178 tragically perished. Harrowing stories of personal tragedies unfolded in statements given and published in great detail in the Liverpool newspapers, when the survivors reached land. Manchester man and printer, Joshua Wilson, with his wife and young daughter in his arms, attempted to use the rope to board the *Affonso*. He made it but sadly his loved ones slipped, fell into the sea and drowned. Anne Taylor of Leeds managed to lower herself, her son and daughter into the water, but the waves washed away the two children.

In the *Mercury,* an unnamed passenger aboard Prince of Wales reported:

> *'Corpses were seen floating past us in considerable numbers. The boats were then immediately lowered and manned. As soon as the men were in the first boat, a poor fellow, quite naked, was seen floating, supported by a life-buoy. They made for him and got him on board. As they were coming alongside the Ocean Monarch a child, two or three years old, was picked up, but life was nearly extinct, and it expired a few minutes after it was taken on board.'*

In the aftermath of the disaster blame and recrimination followed. Captain Murdoch in his statement said the ship's steward informed him of a fire taking hold in a ventilation shaft. Murdoch said he immediately ordered the steward and two other men to attend to the fire. He however soon realised that the fire was now spreading rapidly and that several passengers were panicking and screaming.

With a real sense of confusion spreading, Murdoch said he was losing control. He ordered the boats to be lowered but the crew were only able to lower two into the sea as the others had been engulfed in flames. He ordered anything that could float, such as spars, to be thrown overboard. With the flames now surrounding him Murdoch said he had no option but to jump overboard to save himself. He was able to cling to a spar and was soon rescued by Littledale's yacht.

As for the cause of the fire, Murdoch laid the blame squarely on the steerage passengers. He said the previous evening several them, under strict instructions not to, had been smoking and he confiscated five pipes. He believed this did not prevent passengers smoking on the day of the disaster.

Captain Murdoch's version of events was, nonetheless, contradicted and challenged. His behaviour was criticised by some passengers, including Joshua Wilson and another Manchester man, John Bell. The Liverpool press reported most of the two men's statements, but refused to publish parts that were critical of the captain, though the *Manchester Times* did publish their statements in full.

Wilson said he was on deck watching some of the crew share out tobacco when the steward told the captain of the fire. Wilson said that Murdoch initially took no notice instead ordering the sailors to work on the mast. Only when more crew members alerted the captain of the fire did he react and order some of them to put it out. Captain Murdoch offered no assistance to the problem but stood around swearing at the steerage passengers and blaming them for the fire, Wilson added. He swore a bit more and then disappeared. Wilson, though not witnessing the incident for himself, claimed that it was at that moment the captain threw himself overboard.

Bell, a machine maker, accused Murdoch of cowardice. People had asked the captain what they should do as the flames spread. Bell claimed that Murdoch responded by saying *'do the best for yourselves; I am no longer your captain.'* The captain was, moreover in the opinion of Bell. *'a brute.'* He said Murdoch often swore at and struck the passengers, while on one occasion, when Wilson's child was crying, the captain stamped his foot and ordered its mother to throw the baby overboard.

At a Liverpool inquest into six bodies recovered and returned to the town, Borough Coroner, Philip Finch Curry, offered another explanation for the cause of the fire which had been brought to his attention. Reported in all local newspapers, the coroner informed the inquest that an unnamed seaman claimed that a fellow seaman, Edward Jenkins:

> *'...was seen going into the lazarette* (a store room at the rear of a ship) *with a lighted candle at about 08:00 a.m. and 20 minutes later, coming up without it. About 12:00, smoke was seen issuing from under the cabin which is above the lazarette. The door was broken open and the cabin was found to be on fire. Jenkins was asked where the candle was and he said he had put it in his pocket, to grease his shoes.'*

There was highly combustible material, wine, spirits and straw in the lazarette at the time. This explanation as to the origin of the fire was strengthened by many steerage passengers who asserted that there was no sign of fire in their part of the ship. They were alerted to it later. Finch Curry did not though say that this was the definitive explanation for the cause.

Nevertheless, when the criticism of Murdoch was made public many people, in the form of letters to local papers including the *Mercury* and *Mail*, came to the support of the captain. For example, Thomas Henry, a cabin passenger wrote: *'I could see neither cowardice nor unseamanlike behaviour in his actions.'*

Two other cabin passengers W. Ellis and N. Southward wrote, *'Captain Murdoch acted with great coolness... we believe that had the passengers acted under his directions a great many would have been saved.'* Finally, a letter signed by all the surviving crew and 30 passengers stated:

> *'...we saw not a sign of cowardice in him... he did not leave the ship until all signs of life were at an end.'*

Two other ships, *Cambria* and *Orion*, were in the vicinity at the time of the disaster and their captains too came under criticism for failing to participate in the rescue mission. Captain Hunter of the *Cambria*, the *Cunard* ship which held the Blue Riband in 1845, vigorously defended himself in the press. He was sailing from nearby Bangor north Wales to Liverpool with a ship full of passengers, he explained, and a deck crammed with cattle. In a letter to the *London Illustrated News* he said he sailed passed the *Ocean Monarch* on the morning of the disaster and was about three miles away when he was made aware of the ship being in trouble. He wrote:

> *'I should state that I had two hundred passengers on board, and my decks completely crowded with livestock, which would have rendered it difficult to render assistance at any time, but on this occasion much more so. Had I proceeded to the vessel... there can be little doubt the Cambria would have been placed in great danger. All these circumstances considered I still feel that I should not have been justified in running the risk of sacrificing the lives of those passengers who had entrusted themselves to my care.'*

Hunter also added that he only had enough coal aboard to reach Liverpool.

Captain Hunter and the first mate of the *Orion* were called to give evidence at the Liverpool Inquest. The *Orion* was at sea again under the command of Captain Main who was therefore unavailable to defend his actions. Hunter offered the same explanation he offered in his newspaper letter, whilst the *Orion's* first mate explained that the *Orion* had a full ship and was almost ten miles away at the time. The jury did though censure both captains and conveyed their disapproval of their actions. In its verdict, it stated:

> *'We express our disapprobation of the masters of the two steamers Orion and Cambria, who might, we are led to believe, have rendered most efficient service to the ill-fated people on board.'*

Nobody was ultimately held responsible for the tragedy. The effects of the disaster continued for several weeks after the incident. Within a couple of days, bodies were washed ashore along the north Wales coast. On the 8 September five bodies were recovered on Formby Beach and one on the Isle of Man. During mid-September bodies were washing ashore as far away Blackpool. Some of them were identified and buried where they were recovered, but others were interred as unknown victims.

Instantaneously, charitable efforts to aid the survivors began and thousands of pounds were donated by individuals or raised through special events. People donated as little as one shilling with others contributing up to hundreds of pounds. Shows were put on at Liverpool theatres where, for example, at one show in the Theatre Royal, Williamson Square, £180 was raised. Collections amounting to a total of £350 were taken at local churches.

In 1850, Thomas Littledale, the commodore first on the scene of the disaster, went on to become chairman of the Liverpool Dock Board and Mayor of Liverpool the following year. For his actions, Frederick Jerome was awarded the Freedom of New York on his return to the city.

The *Virginius*

Around 6.20 on the evening of 2 November 1847, travelling on a country lane in a horse-drawn carriage in the Irish county of Roscommon was magistrate, landowner and tenant farmer Major Denis Mahon. He was returning to his home in nearby Strokestown and, as a member of Board of Guardians of the Roscommon Union, he was responsible for the administration of the poor law and the local workhouse. Travelling with Mahon were two other others, his coachman and a close friend, Doctor Terence Shanley.

In the evening darkness two men, armed with pistols, stopped the carriage and approached; two shots rang out and a bullet struck Mahon in the chest; he died within a couple of minutes. Mahon's companions were unhurt and the gunmen escaped into the night.

One newspaper, the Irish *Northern Standard* reporting on the murder on 5 November, described Mahon as:

> *'Not only a kind and indulgent landlord but one who sensitively felt for the distressed situation of his fellow man. He always endeavoured to ameliorate the condition of the people regardless of class or creed.'*

The distressed situation being referred to was the potato famine which, for the previous two years, had ravaged huge swaths of the Irish countryside, killing tens of thousands and forcing many thousands more to emigrate.

In November 1845 (and almost two years to the day), Major Mahon had inherited his grandfather's 11,000 acre Strokestown estate in Roscommon. Thousands of people lived as tenants and worked on the estate at the time. Mahon took ownership in the first catastrophic famine year. According to Dr Ciaran Reilly in an article in an Irish magazine, *The Journal*, of May 2014, Mahon:

> *'...wasn't taking on a fully-functional estate, instead, after years of neglect of the land and mismanagement, it was almost £30,000 in debt, suffering from gross overcrowding and mounting arrears.'*

By 1847, with the famine unrelenting and his tenants unable to pay their rents, Reilly says Mahon came up with a plan to solve his problems. Along with his land agent, they came up with a scheme of *'assisted* emigration'. He would pay the fees of his tenants to emigrate to Canada, which included the hiring of four Liverpool ships to transport them across the Atlantic. The *Northern Standard* praised Mahon for his efforts saying the people on his estate would:

> '...not till the ground or give up possession, so Major Mahon provided them with free passage to travel and food and clothing for the journey.'

Reilly believes it would have cost over £11,000 annually to feed and shelter those needy people should they find themselves in the Roscommon workhouse. However, a one-off emigration scheme would cost around half that at £5,800.

Thus, in May 1847 1,490 tenants left Mahon's Strokestown estate destined for Quebec in Canada; some went willingly and some unwillingly. Frail from hunger and several them weakened and ailing from the onset of typhus, a deadly, highly infectious disease spread by body lice. On the first part of the journey they had to walk 90 miles from Strokestown to Dublin to board a ship to Liverpool. The tenants were accompanied by a bailiff, John Robinson, whom Mahon instructed to stay with across the Irish Sea to ensure they boarded the Mahon hired Canada bound Liverpool ships.

On 28 May 1847, the *Virginius*, the first of the Liverpool hired ships, sailed from its home port for a twelve-week Atlantic passage to Quebec. It was followed over the next couple of weeks by the ships *Naomi, John Munn* and *Erin's Queen*. The ships' port of call in Canada was to be Grosse Ile, the site of an immigration depot established by the Canadian government to deal with cases of cholera and typhus carried by many infected European immigrants. Liverpool ships transporting Irish emigrants had been sailing to Grosse Ile since late spring. The first ship, the *Syria* arrived there on 17 May, initially carrying 253 passengers, but on arrival nine were dead and 53 diagnosed and quarantined as seriously ill.

Other Liverpool ships followed that summer. On 10 August newspaper, the *Cork Examiner*, reported that six Liverpool ships had arrived at Grosse Ile during the summer and all carried typhus fever victims. The *Goliath* sailed with 600 passengers of whom 46 died on the journey; *Jordine* 354 passengers, eight died; *Sarah* 248 passengers, 31 died; *Triton* 448 passengers, 90 died; *Thistle* 389 passengers, eight died; *Manchester 512 passengers,* eleven died. The paper reported that most of the crew and half the passengers of the *Triton* were fever victims. The worst infected ship to make the journey however was soon to arrive at the port.

The *Virginius* docked at Grosse Ile on 12 August and, after a two-week quarantine period, the authorities were horrified at what they discovered. Conditions during the ten-week voyage of the ship were appalling; the *Times* of 17 September described the hold of the ship as *'The Black Hole of Calcutta'*. 158 of the 476 passengers had perished at sea with another 19 dying during the quarantine.

The *Toronto Globe* reported the words of the depot's doctor, George Douglas. He described those who emerged from the ship as *'ghastly, yellow-looking spectres, unshaven and hollow cheeked.'* Douglas, who treated and spoke with the Mahon tenants, noted that some intended emigrants had died in Liverpool, yet the authorities were still prepared to let hundreds of passengers with similar symptoms board the ship. Moreover, it wasn't just the emigrants either that died of fever; all but three crew members lost their lives, including the ship's captain.

Canadians were getting increasingly enraged by the arrival of Liverpool ships on their home shores. On 18 August, the *Liverpool Mail* reported a statement by an angry Montreal Board of Health which asserted:

'Wretched outcasts that have infected that city are shipped from Liverpool. The authorities there have continued to relieve themselves by exporting multitudes to die on the passage or die miserably here' (Canada).

A couple of weeks later, a further report from Douglas appeared in the Globe. He stated:

'Another plague ship has dropped in, the Naomi from Liverpool. This ship sailed on June 15th with 331 passengers, 78 have died on the voyage and 104 are now sick. The filth and dirt in this vessel's hold create such an effluvium as to make it difficult to breathe.'

On Mahon's other hired ships *John Munn* and *Erin's Queen* 59 and 86 respectively were dead on arrival at Grosse Ile.

The emigrant vessels were soon to be characterised as *'coffin ships'* during the famine period. Many similar ships sailed to the USA with similar results. News of the coffin ships spread throughout Ireland. Despite knowing of the horrors, ship owners continued to pack emigrant vessels with disease ridden passengers. In 1847, a total of 72 Liverpool ships arrived in Quebec. It is estimated that by 1849 more than 5,000 Irish immigrants died at Grosse Ile. The isle is said to house the largest famine cemetery outside of Ireland.

Mahon, in his roles as a member of the Board of Guardians, a landowner and magistrate, had, seemingly, made himself a target for assassination. Another Irish newspaper, the *Freeman's Journal*, which was sympathetic to the plight of those suffering from the disastrous effects of the famine, took a different view of Mahon to the *Northern*

Standard. On 30 October, four days before his murder, the paper wrote of the Major:

> *'The people were displeased with him for two reasons; the first was his refusal to continue the conacre system* (the renting of strips of land for an eleven-month period); *the second was his clearing away what he deemed surplus population to America.'*

The *Northern Standard* though disgusted, did agree that Mahon's assassination was popular in the locality. It wrote:

> *'It appears that many of the people of Strokestown were aware of the intended assassination – within one hour of the foul deed several hills were lighted by bonfires in every direction.'*

The authorities were determined not to let the assassins go free. They spent months investigating the case, arresting and detaining many before eventually convicting two men for the crime. On 8 August 1848, Patrick Hasty was executed for conspiracy to murder Major Mahon. At his trial informants gave evidence against Hasty, saying he organised the distribution of pistols to the assassins. Hasty denied involvement in the murder, but on the morning of his execution he signed a declaration admitting and regretting his part.

In February 1849, also principally on the evidence of informants, James Cummins was found guilty of murder. He was judged to be the assassin; the man who fired the shot that killed Denis Mahon. At his trial, he too affirmed his innocence, but like Hasty he also declared his guilt and regret on the morning of his execution.

Almost certainly it would appear that Mahon's policy of assisted emigration played a part in his murder. He, Hasty, Cummins, along with the eventual hundreds of those poor, unfortunate Irish emigrants and the crews of the hired Mahon Liverpool ships, were all essentially though victims of the potato famine.

2. Health and Welfare Campaigns and Campaigners

One of the greatest challenges to the government and local authorities in mid-nineteenth century Britain was public health. Recurring diseases such as cholera and typhoid were commonplace, but knowledge of their origins and spread was in short supply. In Liverpool, the issue of personal cleanliness was uppermost in several people's minds, such as William Rathbone and Kitty Wilkinson, and washing and bathing were promoted by them as a means of attempting to tackle the problem.

Much of Liverpool's overcrowded housing was in a dreadful state. Poor sanitation helped to spread disease and two men, William Henry Duncan and James Newlands, emerged and became determined to try to remedy the dreadful situation, which they did with varying degrees of success. Finally, for some the intake of alcohol was of great concern and the decade saw a real growth in the increase of alcohol abstinence and temperance societies campaigning in the town. Two of the leading figures to surface in the campaign were local man, John Finch and Irish priest Theobald Mathew, whose visits to the town were very popular.

Kitty Wilkinson and William Rathbone: Public Washhouses and Baths

In 1904, St John's Gardens opened in the city centre replacing a church cemetery with a setting of pleasant tranquillity. Situated in the gardens are several statues dedicated to some of Liverpool's historical figures, amongst them William Rathbone. Rathbone, born in 1787, was a merchant and an active partner in the family firm. He was elected a Liberal councillor in Liverpool in 1835 and became the town's Mayor in 1837. He campaigned for many causes including improvement in public health, nursing, temperance and national education. On the plinth below his statue, there are panels in low relief depicting scenes from Rathbone's life including a hospital scene and a domestic scene that suggests a poor couple and children living in poverty.

Inside St. George's Hall, no more than fifty yards from the Rathbone memorial, stands a statue of Kitty Wilkinson, unveiled in 2012 and the first of a woman in that grand location. Wilkinson, born in 1786, is recognised, along with Rathbone, as the originator of Liverpool's first public washhouse and baths. The *Liverpool Echo*, reporting on the unveiling on 21 September 2012, wrote:

> 'Derry-born Kitty, dubbed "saint of the slums", allowed her Liverpool home to be used as a washhouse during cholera epidemics in the 1830s. She opened the first public washhouse in the country, in Upper Frederick Street in 1842, and had a role in teaching people that cholera was linked to dirty water and cleanliness was a weapon against disease.'

Kitty Wilkinson's life and her association with Rathbone have been much written about. Most biographers agree that Kitty had a tough and at times tragic life, so to begin with it is worth looking over a summary of her years, as described by a few sources, in order to assess her efforts in helping to fight against the ravages of a cholera epidemic and her part in establishing the first washhouse.

Her story begins in February 1794 when as an eight-year-old Kitty Seward she, along with her father, mother and younger sister and brother, boarded a Liverpool bound ship in the Irish port of Derry. By the time the ship sailed into Liverpool Bay a violent storm was in progress. The small vessel was violently tossed around and many passengers were washed overboard including Kitty's father and sister who were tragically drowned. A small boat picked up the survivors and Kitty and the rest of her family made it safely into Liverpool.

It was a tragic introduction to their adopted town, but the Seward family had to try to make a life for themselves. They found lodgings in Denison Street in Vauxhall. Kitty's mother eventually found work for herself and daughter as domestic servants. The tragedy though had taken a serious toll on Kitty's mother who showed signs of mental health problems and became a burden on the family.

Two years later Mrs. Seward decided to return to Ireland and the family's employer suggested the children be sent away to work; consequently, Kitty and her brother were removed to the small village of Caton in Lancashire to work in a cotton mill. There the siblings stayed and worked for the next ten years. It was a happy life and Kitty met her future second husband, Tom, for the first time at the mill.

In 1812 Kitty returned to Liverpool to join her mother who had also reappeared in the town and both once again were employed as domestic servants. In the same year, she met a French sailor by the name of Emmanuel De Monte who became her first husband. They had their first child the following year. Tragedy however was about to strike again. De Monte went back to the sea. It was 1815 and Kitty was now pregnant with their second child. Emmanuel had reached Canada and Kitty said he wanted to return to see his new child however tragedy was to strike her yet again as Emmanuel's ship sank and he was drowned on his return to Liverpool.

Now a widow she continued to work in domestic service when in 1823 once again she met Tom Wilkinson, now working for the Rathbone family as warehouseman in Liverpool. They soon married. Kitty now wanted a change to her working life and, as a literate person she decided to put her skills to use. In 1825 she opened a day school in her home. She taught reading, writing and sewing to up to ten children per session who paid three pennies for the service. However, Kitty's mother was proving troublesome. She was prone to fits of temper and constantly disrupted the lessons Kitty taught. Kitty felt that the school could no longer be maintained and five years after it opened it was closed.

Liverpool author Michael Kelly *(The Life and Times of Kitty Wilkinson: 2000)* writes that Kitty and Tom were living in Denison Street on the eve of the 1832 cholera epidemic and:

> '...they were involved in helping the community. Kitty continued to be called upon to nurse the sick and when she was not nursing took in orphans from the street.'

After closing the school Kitty chose to return to domestic service. Part of this included laundry work and she was able to purchase a hot water boiler situated in her kitchen where she washed the clothes and bedding of her neighbours. She sometimes worked for up to 23 hours per day. Despite her strenuous efforts and Tom's warehouse work the family struggled for survival, some days eating only a bowl of gruel. When Kitty did have a surplus of money she often gave it away to her needier neighbours.

In 1832 the cholera epidemic sweeping Europe reached Liverpool; the consequences of which were disastrous for the town. Between 12 May and 13 September there were 4,977 cases, of which 1,523 proved fatal. On 5 October, the city was declared free of the epidemic. Whilst the cholera ravaged the town, Kitty worked night and day to aid her neighbours in trying to combat the deadly effects of the disease. She visited medical officers for advice. She cared little for her own welfare; all that mattered was the protection of her family and neighbours. The Wilkinsons also took in some of the local orphan children whose parents had died of cholera.

Though the exact date is unclear, local charity the District Provident Society, of which Rathbone was a leading member became involved and installed another boiler in Kitty's cellar. On 22 August 1840 during a council debate on the plans for the establishment of a washhouse and reported in the *Liverpool Mercury*, Rathbone described events:

> *'The instances were frequent where Cholera or fever seemed to have taken possession of a house, and when, after a complete washing of bed, bedding and clothes and whitewashing the room, not another instance of infection occurred... In no single instance was there reason to think that the means taken were not completely successful in purifying the clothes, and preserving from contagion those who washed them... in one week in August 1832 - were washed for those ill of Cholera – 158 sheets, 110 blankets, 60 quilts, 34 bed-ticks and 140 dozen of clothes. The dirty state of the clothes, in most cases of fever, told plainly the common origin of the disease, which was confirmed by the striking exemption from fever of those families who regularly washed in the cellar.'*

It is unclear exactly when, but Kitty probably met Rathbone and his wife Elizabeth at sometime either during or after the epidemic. In a report of 1856 *(The Frederick Street Washhouse)* City Engineer, James Newlands, praised the combined efforts of the three:

'The great supporters of Mrs. Wilkinson in her praiseworthy efforts were Mr. and Mrs. William Rathbone. To their fostering care, we owe the recognition of her services and the institutions to which they gave rise. Here, then, was the germ of the public washhouse institutions.'

After the epidemic Kitty went on to work for the District Provident Society until 1837 when again afterwards she returned to work in domestic service.

* * * * *

At the turn of the decade, Councillor Rathbone energetically campaigned for the introduction of public baths and washhouses, as evidenced in his speech above. Though defeated in the council elections of November 1840, he continued to campaign outside the council chamber. It took months of hard work as the council was split with many Tories in opposition, but eventually council colleagues of Rathbone in favour of the plans were able to convince enough members to support the proposals.

The council gave its approval for the construction of the first public washhouse and baths on Upper Frederick Street. The building was opened on 28 May 1842. The superintendents of the newly opened facility however were Andrew Clarke and his wife and not Kitty and Tom Wilkinson. One reason for this may have been the fact that Rathbone had lost his council seat and therefore had no influence on the decision. The Wilkinsons had applied, along with 103 other married couples, for the publicly advertised positions, but a committee of four councillors chose the Clarkes from a shortlist of four.

Within a few weeks of their opening, Upper Frederick Street Baths and Washhouses were declared a success. J. Calvert (*'The means of cleanliness'; the provision of baths and washhouses in early Victorian Liverpool in Transactions of the Lancashire and Cheshire Historical Societies, 1987*) writes:

> *'There simply was not enough room to accommodate all the people wishing to use the facilities. The washhouses, and especially the drying area, were not extensive enough. 27,984 baths were taken in the first two years; and 44,696 dozens of clothes were washed; the numbers continued to increase as the statistics from 1842 to 1846 show, and the Council therefore resolved to erect a building 'of greater extent, with the improved accommodation, arrangement and appliances that experience showed to be advisable.'*

There was however a tragedy to report from the facility. In December 1842, the Clarkes' two-year-old son fell into one of the filled bathing tubs and tragically drowned.

* *

In 1845, Rathbone returned to the council as a member for Vauxhall and the following year a second washhouse was opened in that ward in Paul St. The Clarkes were transferred and became superintendents of the new facility. Rathbone then made a special plea on behalf of Kitty that she and Tom take charge of the Upper Frederick Street Washhouse. On 1 July, reported in the *Mercury* on 4 July, he distributed a testimonial on behalf of the Wilkinsons and addressed the council. He admitted to operating outside the committee responsible for appointments saying:

'The singularity of the case must be my excuse for bringing the application of Mr. and Mrs. Wilkinson for the situation of superintendents of the baths and washhouses in Frederick Street, before the members of the town council in this uncommon manner.'

He spoke of Kitty's *'talents for management and economy'* and her *'fearlessness'* during the cholera outbreak. On 7 July Rathbone was appointed to the sub-committee of five councillors given the responsibility of appointing the Upper Frederick Street superintendents. The five discussed twelve applications and the committee shortlisted three before finally recommending to the full council that Kitty and Thomas Wilkinson be appointed to the posts.

Kitty at the time was highly praised in some sections of the Liverpool press. On 15 January 1847, the *Mercury* reprised her labours for its readers. The paper wrote of her *'unwearied efforts to assist her poor neighbours with daily visits and nightly attendances of the sick and the dying.'* It went on to compare her efforts with Grace Darling, the lighthouse keeper's daughter, famed for participating in the rescue of survivors from a shipwreck in 1838, and the prisoner reformer Elizabeth Fry. On 26 January 1848 Rathbone, responding to requests regarding the origins of the washhouses, wrote to various publications including the *Economist* and mentioned:

'... a poor woman, the wife of a labourer used a boiler in her kitchen... she was aided by the District Provident Society.'

* *

In the twentieth century, Kitty was described as the *'Saint of the Slums,'* as in the *Echo* description above. Liverpool historian, Richard Whittington-Egan, was one of the first to call Kitty *'saintly'* in his effulgent praise of her in *Liverpool Characters and Eccentrics* (1968). He claimed that Kitty *'became the ministering angel of the epidemic.* Adding:

'She contributed sheets and blankets for sick beds from her own slender stock and placed her tiny kitchen, which contained a boiler, at the disposal of her neighbours so that they might wash and disinfect with chloride of lime those disease-laden clothes and bedding.

Producer of the most detailed biography of Kitty, Michael Kelly says she worked continuously to fight the ravages of the cholera. Writing, for example:

'With the help of her husband, Kitty worked day and night to try to combat the nightmare that had erupted all around them. The signs of what was to come must have been all too clear to Kitty, for she had been actively involved with those who were homeless and sick for most of her life... she was a true Christian... being in need was the only qualification that mattered to her.'

Many other articles and references to her life in Liverpool history books, have been as equally praiseworthy.

From where do the sources for all the praise bestowed upon Kitty emerge? Apart from the Rathbones, how do we know of her early life and the later work she did in trying to combat the cholera epidemic? A trawl of the local press at the time of the cholera epidemic does not refer to her work. If she visited medical men for advice this may well have been of interest to local reporters keen for their readership to be informed of unfolding events. Throughout 1832 the papers did report regularly from the cholera hospital based in the infirmary on Lime Street (now St George's Hall). It could be that they chose to ignore the work of a working-class woman, with no qualifications to back her efforts.

Kitty did though have the support of the District Provident Society with its wealthy benefactors such as members of the Rathbone family, so why did they not attempt to publicise her efforts during the epidemic rather than inform the public of it a decade or so later? Indeed, the society's 1833 annual report, produced in May for the year ending in April, also failed to mention anything about Kitty's work. In fact, there is only a trivial reference to the cholera epidemic itself in the final paragraph.

Despite all her exertions Kitty's name would not have been widely known to the public until the 1840s. At this period, Rathbone was formulating his case for the establishment of the washhouses. As is evidenced from some of Rathbone's tributes, his manner in praising Kitty was not always clear. In his August 1840 address to the council, on the need for washhouses, he praised the efforts of the work carried out at a laundry on Upper Frederick Street. However, he failed to mention Kitty's name.

There is therefore much confusion as to where the couple lived. One reason for this could be that according to contemporary sources Kitty was not living in Upper Frederick Street at the time but her husband Tom was. Gore's Liverpool Street Directory names Kitty (Catherine) living in Denison Street in the early 1830s. She is registered as a *'Lodging House Keeper.'* Meanwhile according to the same source at the same time a Thomas Wilkinson is living in Upper Frederick Street registered as a *'warehouseman.'* At the end of the decade, he is described as a *'coal dealer.'*

Kitty does not appear in the directory living in Denison Street after 1837. It is highly probable that the Thomas Wilkinson of Upper Frederick Street is Kitty's husband for two reasons; Thomas was a warehouseman and the 1841 census reveals a Thomas and Catherine Wilkinson residing in Upper Frederick Street.

Only when the second washhouse required a superintendent in 1846 did Rathbone really name and praise Kitty and Tom in the manner we know of today. In support of their application he said in his letter and address to the council that:

> *'...their active benevolence and fearlessness of infection are very uncommon and it only by such that the washing of infected clothes will be carried out to its full capability. I am anxious about it for its effect upon the poor, as encouragement to follow her example.'*

The *Mercury*, an ardent supporter of Rathbone, reporting on 4 July 1846, not only printed his words but also heaped further praise upon Kitty stating that she was the *'originator of the washhouses.'*
Much of Kitty's life did not come to notice until 1927, following the publication of the *Memoir of Kitty Wilkinson* by Herbert R Rathbone a great nephew of William and Elizabeth. The author of the foreword to the book, Irish Nationalist MP TP O'Connor, admitted to not having heard of Kitty until approached to pen the preamble.

The memoir is based on material left by Elizabeth Rathbone and discovered in her belongings after her death. Herbert says the material is from an unknown author but it is hard not to believe that it was authored by Elizabeth or Kitty herself. Herbert writes that

Elizabeth visited Kitty on a regular basis after the cholera epidemic and recorded many of their conversations, eventually summarising them in 1835.

Therefore, the clear majority of what we know of Kitty's life before this date must originate from Kitty herself. She is very much the primary and only source of her early life. She is working from memory to tell of her early years and consequently mistakes will have been made. For example, contemporary sources, such as Lloyd's of London (established to provide insurance for shipping) provides no reference to a shipwreck occurring in Liverpool Bay in February 1794 and certainly not of a ship sailing from Derry. The closest catastrophe to that date was the sinking of a Liverpool bound Dublin ship, the *St Patrick,* on 25 January 1794 off the coast of Anglesey in which four unnamed passengers tragically drowned. Two of those killed may well have been Kitty's father and sister and it would be easy to make errors after such a traumatic incident.

Similarly, there are no recorded sinkings of British bound ships sailing from Canada in 1815. How could have Kitty possibly have known at the time that her husband intended to leave Canada to sail home to his family? Communication across continents 200 years ago, was incredibly difficult.

Did Emmanuel De Monte leave her as a single mother with two children? Did Kitty have to tell people that her husband had drowned so she could move on with her life? Kitty would have faced enormous pressure living life as single, deserted mother in the early nineteenth century.

Whatever Kitty's memory or motivations it appears that Elizabeth Rathbone dutifully noted the information furnished to her by Kitty.

When it came to the cholera epidemic, Kitty may have told Elizabeth that her work was motivated by a conviction to combat the disease. Few, if any, at the time knew of the origins and how cholera spread (see Duncan below) and the best methods to deal with its effects. Kitty's description of her work then could be praised without much contradiction. This would have proved useful for William Rathbone to promote his idea and plan for public washhouses and baths.

Was it necessarily a bad thing that Rathbone used Kitty Wilkinson's work to gain support the idea for the kind of facilities he proposed to aid the health and wellbeing of the Liverpool public? If it helped his case, then it was certainly effective. After all his washhouse and baths provision came into effect. Not everybody on the council supported him or his idea so why not praise, or even exaggerate, the efforts of a *'poor, working class woman'* to achieve your aims? Turn what was in effect Kitty's home laundry service, assisted by the District Provident Society, into a concerted effort to combat cholera. Having used Kitty's work to shore up his case, the least Rathbone could do in return was to support her application to become superintendent at Upper Frederick Street.

The combination of William's Rathbone's praise and Herbert Rathbone's memoir has contributed to the modern image of Kitty Wilkinson. To repeat the words of the *Echo*:

> *'Kitty allowed her Liverpool home to be used as a washhouse during cholera epidemics in the 1830s. She opened the first public washhouse in the country, in Upper Frederick Street in 1842.'*

Doubt must be cast upon the first part of that statement (she was a laundress anyway) and the latter part of it is certainly not true. Kitty not only did not open the washhouse; the council did not appoint her as its first superintendent.

To conclude with Kitty Wilkinson's life, less than two years after her and her husband became superintendents at Upper Frederick Street, tragedy was to strike her yet again. Tom died of bronchitis on 31 December 1847, barely 17 months after his appointment. Kitty submitted a request to the council's health committee to be allowed to continue the superintendence of the washhouse and baths, with the assistance of her son. The council acceded to her request and she retained her post, but only until 1851 when, owing to demand upon the services, the building closed in order to be replaced by a superior facility also built on Upper Frederick Street. She was kept on as caretaker for a further year and then as a mender of towels at which she worked until her death on 11 November 1860, aged 73. She is buried in St James' cemetery.

Her headstone can still be seen today and she is permanently commemorated in a stained-glass window in the Anglican Cathedral, which honours the noble women of Liverpool and, of course, there is the statue to her in St. George's Hall.

Housing, Epidemics and Sanitation: Dr William Henry Duncan and James Newlands

Perhaps the most famed individual credited with endeavouring to improve the health and wellbeing of Liverpool's citizens is William Henry Duncan. A physician and medical officer of health, Duncan's major concern was the overcrowded court and cellar housing, poor sanitation and the seemingly endless reoccurrence of epidemic diseases such as cholera and typhus.

Duncan was born in Seel Street on 27 January 1805, the fifth of the seven children of George Duncan, a Liverpool merchant and his wife, Christian. Of Scottish heritage, Duncan chose from 1825 to study medicine at Edinburgh University. He graduated in 1829 and returned to Liverpool to begin practicing medicine, serving as a physician at the Central and North dispensaries. Furthering his career from 1835 he lectured at the Liverpool Royal Institution School of Medicine and Surgery (which became the Liverpool Infirmary in 1844). He went on to become a physician at Liverpool's Northern Hospital from 1837.

The 1832 cholera epidemic became of particular interest and a cause of major concern for Duncan. He was determined to learn of its causes and how and why the disease spread. Duncan believed there was a distinct correlation between the disease and environment, in particular the habitation of the poor living principally in overcrowded courts and cellars. He concluded that cholera was transmitted by *miasma*,' an oppressive or unpleasant atmosphere which surrounds or emanates from something, usually rotting or decaying.

In the case of the cholera epidemic for Duncan, miasma was spread by human and animal waste as well as discarded rotting food products. He concluded therefore that ventilation, and the circulation of fresh air, was crucial towards improving people's health.

At the turn of the decade, Duncan spent a great deal of his time visiting the courts and cellars of Liverpool's poorest districts to collect evidence for a report he hoped to submit to parliament. He was eventually invited to deliver that report in person in 1840. With miasma at the forefront of his conclusions, he informed the House of Commons' select committee on the health of towns that he believed the principal circumstances affecting the health of the poor were:

- Imperfect ventilation
- Want of places of deposit for animal waste and vegetable refuse
- Imperfect drainage and sewerage
- Imperfect system of scavenging (street sweeping) and cleansing

He added that he believed individual habits increased the causes of fever, including:

- Their tendency to congregate in too large numbers under one roof
- Want of cleanliness
- Indisposition to be removed to hospital when ill of fever

In the report, Duncan was especially scathing of the Irish. Evidently blaming the victims, he said:

'It is they who inhabit the filthiest and worst ventilated courts and cellars... that are the least cleanly in their habits... It is amongst the Irish that fever especially commits its ravages... they are rapidly lowering the standard and comfort of their English neighbours, communicating their own vicious and apathetic habits.'

He concluded that fever will never disappear whilst the Irish arrive *'spreading physical and moral contamination.'* He made no mention of poverty as a factor in the report. One final recommendation made by Duncan stated that he believed that decreasing the mortality rate in Liverpool would be assisted if:

'...an efficient plan of inspection was carried into effect; if power were invested in some officer or board to investigate the dwellings of the poor.'

Returning to Liverpool, over the following couple of years he continued to survey housing conditions in the town. He discovered a third of the population lived in the cellars of larger houses, most of which had earth floors and no ventilation or sanitation, (the cellars were never meant as living accommodation but rather for storage). He further discovered as many as 16 people living in a single room.

Duncan published a report in 1843 titled, *'On the Physical Causes of the high rate of mortality in Liverpool'* which became particularly influential. In it he declared Liverpool to be *'the most unhealthy town in England.'* He identified that around half of children died before they were two years old and therefore, in 1841, the average age of death in the town was just 17 years of age. He did though in this report recognise poverty as a probable factor in poor health. He said that the Irish population of Liverpool *'did tend to reside in the poorest parts of the town.'*

The report contained several recommendations including regulating the building of courts (these were usually closed off, but now had to be open at one end to allow air to circulate) and the demolition of their worst types; the prevention of the habitation of cellars and, with respect to Liverpool, a promotion of a private health bill to be presented to parliament.

Duncan's concerted efforts led the council to introduce the Liverpool Sanitary Act 1846. The act established a public health service and on 1 January 1847 Liverpool became the first town or city in the world to employ a Medical Officer of Health when it appointed Duncan to a part time post. He was upgraded to a full time official in 1848 at an annual salary of £750; he had now the substantial powers he had recommended in his 1840 report. He was given authority to inspect and report on sanitary conditions of all forms of housing.

* *

The month after Duncan's appointment, Liverpool council employed James Newlands as the world's first municipal engineer. Newlands, born in Edinburgh in 1813, studied mathematics and natural philosophy at the city's university and became an architect for the council. One of five candidates for the post, Newlands went on to head Edinburgh University's School of Agriculture, where he was rewarded with a salary of £700 a year.

Christopher Hamlin, (*James Newlands and the bounds of public health: Transactions of the Historic Society of Lancashire and Cheshire. 1993*), states that Newlands next appointment as Liverpool's Engineer came about despite him: '*having little experience in matters of sewerage, drainage, street paving, or other of the duties of municipal engineers.*'

Working alongside Duncan, Newlands is credited with designing and implementing the first integrated sewerage system in the world in 1848. Observing that human waste was often found lying in the street aiding the spread of disease. Duncan decreed that only a properly organised system of sewerage could combat this particular problem. Engineer Newlands was the man with the knowledge and expertise to undertake this enormous task. He first set about making a careful and exact survey of Liverpool streets and surrounding countryside. This resulted in the creation of a town map whereby he could plan a comprehensive system of sewers and drains.

In July 1848, Newlands' construction programme began, and over the next eleven years 86 miles of new sewers and drains were built. Liverpool council installed dozens of fresh water hydrants too. In addition, 33 scavengers, working to clear the streets of human waste, were employed. By 1850, the number had increased to 400. Meanwhile, Duncan was implementing further changes he believed were required to improve the health of Liverpool's population. Although facing opposition, he robustly defended his actions. For example, with respect to housing, Duncan hated the use of storage cellars for living accommodation. He and his team toured the town re-inspecting the inhabited cellars and eventually ordered more than 5,000 of them (out of 7,688) to be cleared. By the end of the decade, more than 20,000 individuals had been displaced from cellars. This drastic action led to criticism as Duncan did not appear to consider where the banished were expected to live.

Arguably, though, Duncan's principal challenge was the reoccurrence of epidemic disease. He took up his post in 1847 in the year of the largest influx of Irish people fleeing the ravages of the potato famine and a year that evidenced a return of typhus (which Duncan and many others referred to somewhat unfairly as *'Irish Fever'*). At the end of that year, Liverpool suffered 5,845 deaths from the fever with an additional 2,589 dying from diarrhoea.

Duncan reported that over 100,000 more had shown symptoms of these illnesses, but survived. He also learned that deaths spread disproportionately across the town. The poorest ward, Vauxhall, suffered a death rate of one in seven of its residents. By comparison, the wealthier ward of Rodney Street and Abercromby Square the rate was one in 35.

Nevertheless, it was his theory on the spread of cholera that proved problematical for Duncan. Typhus was the other major killer disease devastating towns and cities. Transmitted to humans via parasites such as lice, ticks and fleas, symptoms began with sudden onset of fever, chills, headache and other flu-like symptoms. A couple of weeks following infection the victim developed a rash that began to spread. This rash eventually covered the entire body resulting in death for the worst sufferers after about three weeks. Typhus killed people of all classes, as lice were endemic and almost unavoidable, but it hit especially hard the working class without access to clean, hot water. Duncan though doubted that typhus was also a contagious disease spread by human contact.

Cholera returned in 1849 killing 5,245 Liverpool citizens. Symptoms of this disease included the victim suffering from diarrhoea, vomiting and muscle cramps. Diarrhoea was so severe that within hours severe dehydration occurred and death quickly followed. Duncan and his team visited many homes that year in which a death from cholera occurred. A reporter from the *Liverpool Journal* undertook a similar journey he called *'A Walk around the Cholera Districts'* which the newspaper published on 4 November 1849. A sample of his evidence (similar to what no doubt Duncan witnessed) revealed the misery cholera inflicted on many Liverpool citizens:

'Oriel Street (off Vauxhall Road): one side of the street had suffered no fatalities, but some courts on the other side yielded a significant proportion of lamentable deaths. There are cellars too damp and too offensive even for storage, serving hitherto, to generate disease.'

'In Addison Street (close to Tithebarn Street) the cholera raged in every house taking off 30 people. Some children left helpless, still occupying the house where their father died.'

'To Toxteth Park and Henderson Street where the cholera had been bad. They were by no means the worst courts in the area, but in

one house, to which a filthy passage was access, here the cholera carried off a man named McKee, his wife, mother and daughter.'

The epidemic delivered Duncan the biggest challenge to his theory of miasma. He did not believe cholera to be contagious, but a disease that spread in overcrowded conditions and a toxic atmosphere created by all kinds of waste products. It is now believed the miasma theory largely failed cholera victims.

Cholera was at its deadliest in summer. Historians Gerry Kearns, Paul Laxton, and Joy Campbell *(Duncan and the cholera test: public health in mid nineteenth-century Liverpool: Transactions of the Historic Society of Lancashire and Cheshire, 1993)* say that Duncan claimed that this *'was due to the electricity in the warm atmosphere.'* The warmth he said could produce cholera clouds that drifted around. For example, in 1847 he *'recommended that ships leaving Liverpool avoid the Irish coast as they may pass under cholera clouds.'* Thus, Duncan believed the circulation of clean, fresh air was paramount in dealing with the spread of the disease.

The 1849 epidemic, however, strongly challenged Duncan's hypothesis. He and Newlands had begun to implement their plans for tackling poor housing and poor sanitation, but the cholera epidemic appeared to be ignoring his theory. Despite the sanitary improvements people were dying of the disease. He moved some way to contemplate the idea that cholera could be contagious in certain circumstance. On 2 November 1849, in a letter to the *Mercury*, he wrote:

'Cholera is contagious in certain cases but this is the exception and not the rule. Many washerwomen residing in healthier parts of the town, to whom the linen of cholera patients had been sent, died.'

Kearns, Laxton and Campbell claim that Duncan was probably reluctant to advance the idea of contagion, because of the damage it may have inflicted upon the town. They write:

> '...as a local official, Duncan was keen to avoid stirring up fears of contagion... The broader fear of contagion in foreign ports meant that at the first mention of cholera being in town, epidemic or not, the foreign consuls sent back to their countries the newspaper reports of the Health Committee's weekly counts of deaths and Liverpool ships were subjected to quarantine and all manner of people avoided coming to town to do business.'

In the 1850s, Duncan was still claiming that cholera was not a contagious disease. It took the work of London Doctor John Snow during the 1854 epidemic. He identified the source of the outbreak as a public water pump in Soho, in which a broken sewage pipe leaked into the drinking water supply. His observation led him to discount the theory of miasma. Initially his findings were controversial and not accepted by most medical practitioners until 1866, during yet another outbreak of cholera. His findings inspired fundamental changes in the water and waste systems of London, which led to similar changes in other cities and a significant improvement in general public health.

Despite his mistaken theory on cholera, Duncan's work is, however much lauded as too were the efforts of Newlands. The two men undoubtedly helped to improve the health and wellbeing of the citizens of Liverpool. Their influence and subsequent actions by the council resulted in a significant reduction in the population living in the nastiest cellars and other unhealthy dwellings such as the courts. The demolition of the worst court housing and their replacement by relatively more spacious accommodation certainly helped.

The sewerage system and the employment of scavengers improved immensely the sanitation of the town. There was unquestionably a general improvement in environmental hygiene. For example, at the time of Duncan's death in 1863 in the average age of mortality in Liverpool had risen to 27. He died in Elgin, Scotland on 23 May 1863 whilst visiting family. One of the buildings of the Faculty of Medicine at the University of Liverpool is dedicated to Duncan and the university created a health-debating group, the Duncan Society, in 1999. A pub in Liverpool called *Doctor Duncan's* is named in his honour too.

Newlands went on to write several books in which he recommended the building of public parks and promenades. He did though believe that the building of public baths (not swimming pools) allowed private builders to abrogate their responsibility. He believed that house builders be compelled to construct homes with baths. Hamlin says Newlands was *'A young man with a socialist vision.'* He was too a contributor to the *Encyclopaedia Britannica.* After long bouts of ill health, Newlands died in Liverpool in 1871, aged 57. There is a plaque dedicated to him in Abercromby Square.

John Finch and Theobald Mathew: Temperance

The first temperance societies were formed in the UK in 1829 in Dublin, Glasgow and Belfast. The following year John Finch formed the first society in Liverpool. The early societies opposed the drinking of spirits but were more comfortable with the drinking of beer and wine in moderation. In Preston in 1832 however, the 'Total Abstinence Society' was formed and Finch more of a believer in this initiative formed a branch in Liverpool.

Driven by concerns with what they believed was the connection between poverty, squalor, irreligion and the consumption of alcohol, the proponents of total abstinence spread their influence. The Church of England opened a branch in Liverpool 1837, which had both youth, and senior branches. Whilst in the same year Irishman and ardent teetotaller, James McKenna formed the Liverpool Catholic Total Abstinence Society. Sectarianism was put to one side when it came to abstinence. In the same year, however Finch was expelled from The Total Abstinence Society because *'his words were not in accordance with the word of God.'* Finch declared himself a socialist and believed, rather than religion, that it was necessary to change society to achieve a temperate nation.

At the turn of the decade, with over 2,500 drinking establishments in the town, temperance was growing in popularity. Liverpool had held temperance festivals in the recent past, but in July 1841, such was its attractiveness, the temperance societies put on a weeklong series of events. The festival began on Monday 12 July with thousands attending a march that culminated at St Luke's Church. This was followed the following evening by a mass meeting at the *Amphitheatre* on Charlotte Street and three open air gatherings over the following three nights on Lime Street, St George's Place and London Road. Halls and hotels dedicated to the movement sprang up in abundance throughout the town.

Finch, despite his disputes with the movement remained a fervent advocate. Opening in 1840, he was instrumental in building the *Liverpool Hall of Science* in Lord Nelson Street. The hall was a few doors from a temperance coffee house. It played host to several temperance meetings and entertainment shows with temperance themes. One show in 1841, advertised in the press as *'a combination of sober and rational amusements for the smallest possible expense,'* was typical. The entertainment consisted of different forms of music and comedy at the *'soiree.'*

There were plays and other forms of entertainment dedicated to temperance performed at other venues such as the *Amphitheatre* on Great Charlotte Street. In July 1843, the theatre hosted two plays, advertised in the Mercury on 7th as *'The new gorgeous temperance spectacles'*, entitled *The Bright Star of Temperance* and *The Doomed Ship of the Drunkard.*

Other organisations were too committed to temperance including, for example, some of the early dockworkers' trade unions and associated workers. The Operative Porters, for instance, met at a temperance hall in Marylebone, off Vauxhall Road. On 23 November 1846, the purpose-built Clarence Temperance Hall, Clarence Street, opened. The cost of the building, raised through £1 shares, was £3,500. Hotels such as the Brown's Temperance, where the US anti–slavery campaigner Frederick Douglass stayed in 1847, opened in Clayton Square.

The most famous advocate of temperance during the period arrived in Liverpool in the summer of 1843. Despite having a brewery owning brother, Father Theobald Mathew, born in Ireland in 1790 and ordained a priest in Dublin in 1813 was drawn towards temperance. In 1835, Quaker, William Martin, founder of the Cork Total Abstinence Society, was aware of Father Mathew, who was gaining a reputation as he travelled across Ireland spreading the gospel of temperance. John Finch toured Ireland twice in 1834 and 1836 where he met and was also greatly impressed with the advocacy of Mathew.

In 1838, Martin and Mathew met and the latter signed up to the ideal and plunged headfirst into the abstinence crusade. He quickly earned the nickname *'The Apostle of Temperance'* travelling the country encouraging and converting people to take *'The Pledge'* to remain abstinent from alcohol. Mathew's reputation quickly spread throughout the rest of the UK and he received demands to appear in towns and cities up and down the land. On the eve of his departure to Liverpool, Mathew converted hundreds of Irishmen and women at a public meeting in Dublin, including over 30 of the country's MPs. It is estimated that hundreds of thousands of Irish men and women had taken the pledge by the time of Mathews visit and tour of England, Scotland and Wales in 1843.

Mathew agreed to visit Liverpool following an invitation by the *Total Abstinence Society*, to address its ninth festival at the Liver Theatre, Church Street, on Saturday 15 July. Three days prior to his appearance, the society held a meeting at the same venue, but fewer than 200 people attended, leaving the organisation very concerned that Mathew's visit would prove to be something of a disaster. It need not have worried. On 21 July, the *Mercury* reported that the hall, including many local dignitaries such as William Rathbone and Edward Rushton, was packed to the rafters with many locked out. Mathew said *'My heart has been cheered by the great spread of teetotalism in Liverpool.'*

Mathew, who appropriately stayed at *Brown's Temperance Hotel*, spent the following days administering the pledge in churches and schools, including the *Hibernian School* founded in 1807 in Clarence Street which later became *Pleasant Street Board School*. Everyone administered received a specially designed medal bearing Mathew's name and image to prove to family and friends that they were now temperate.

He spent the final two days of his visit at St Anthony's Church, Scotland Road. On the first morning at the church, he delivered a sermon and following this, with thousands waiting, he commenced the administration of the pledge. The numbers overwhelmed Mathew and, after a few hours, local churchmen had to relieve him of his duty and continued his work on until 10 p.m. that night. Mathew returned the following day to repeat his message and work. By the end of the second day, the *Mercury* estimated that over 20,000 had taken the pledge at the church. The paper also said that it believed that more than 35,000 in total had done so across the town.

On 24 July, in a surprising twist on the Father Mathew phenomenon, *The Times* published a story headlined *'Father Mathew Miracle Worker.'* The paper reported that Mathew had performed a *'miracle'* whilst at St Anthony's. A woman had appeared in front of Mathew with her 14-year-old son who *'had lost the use of his limbs.'* Father Mathew made the sign of the cross over the oy *'and repeated a few words whereupon the boy's legs acquired their long-lost vigour and he actually walked home.'*

The paper added the story would not have had much credence and would have been viewed as superstitious if the *'only witnesses would have been the poor and uneducated.'* The story was though, *The Times* said, repeated: *'by persons in the middle class of life.'* One unnamed person, the report concluded: *'who was not easily deceived, declared that he himself was a witness to the performance of a miracle.'*

Mathew's stay attracted all kinds of attention, which included some who tried to benefit financially from his visit. On 25 August, an advertisement from B. Hyam, a tailor of Lord Street, appeared on the front page of the *Liverpool Mail,* and other newspapers. The advert, published in the form of a poem, praised Father Mathew, and suggested that those who became teetotal would now be able to afford nice, new clothes. One stanza read:

> 'Then would you save money to thee I propose
> B Hyam and Co should make all your clothes'

The movement felt Mathew's visit a huge success. The following year, however, the Liverpool temperance and abstinence societies received correspondence from Mathew's personal secretary, James McKenna. He wrote requesting of them a donation towards the 20,000 or so medals distributed by Mathew. The bill for the medals, manufactured at the churchman's own expense for about one penny each, still needed paying for. On 11 November 1844, the *Mercury,* in an article headed *'The Embarrassments of the Father Mathew Temperance Societies',* reported on a meeting in the school hall of St Anthony's Total Abstinence Society that had managed to *'raise £11 to send over to Ireland.'*

A much bigger meeting of the Liverpool Temperance Society took place a day later at the Assembly Rooms on Lord Nelson Street. The meeting, attended by around 300 including William Rathbone and William Brown, raised £71 from entrance fees. The total garnered by both meetings would have been close enough to cover the cost of the medals. Rathbone nevertheless told the meeting that Father Mathew was in a *'position of pecuniary difficulties'* and further funds should be raised and sent on to Ireland.

A committee was formed, with Rathbone as chairperson, with the aim of drawing together donors who would pledge an amount of money. This was relatively successful and the *Mercury* published a list of donors and their donations (Rathbone and Brown both donated £10 each) which totalled £135 (real price in 2016 about £11,000). The *Mercury* was to be the recipient of any further donations and stated it would pass them on to William Rathbone.

Father Mathew departed Liverpool in the summer of 1843 and travelled the UK for three months converting an estimated 600,000 people to the temperance movement. At the invitation of William Rathbone, he returned to Liverpool in 1849 for his final visit to the town. Before leaving to tour America, he spent a couple of days administering the pledge and calling into Catholic schools to speak to the children of Irish immigrants who had arrived in Liverpool because of the Great Famine.

Temperance and Travel

Many historians believe that Liverpool and temperance play a part in the development of the modern tourist industry. On 9 June 1841, a 32-year old cabinet-maker walked from his home in Market Harborough to the nearby town of Leicester to attend a temperance meeting. The former Baptist preacher was a religious man who believed that most Victorian social problems bore a distinct relationship with alcohol and that the lives of working people would be greatly improved if they drank less (or totally abstained) and became better educated.

As he walked the road to Leicester, he later recalled, *'the thought suddenly flashed across my mind as to the practicability of employing the great powers of railways and locomotion for the furtherance of this social reform.'* That man was Thomas Cook whose name lives on through the holiday company he established. According to the Thomas Cook website:

> 'At the meeting, he suggested that a special train be engaged to carry the temperance supporters of Leicester to a meeting in Loughborough about four weeks later. The proposal was received with such enthusiasm that, on the following day, Thomas submitted his idea to the secretary of the Midland Railway Company.'

A train was subsequently arranged, and on 5 July 1841, about 500 passengers were conveyed to their destination. During the next three summers, Cook arranged a succession of trips from Leicester to Nottingham, Derby and Birmingham on behalf of local temperance societies. When he learned of Father Mathew's forthcoming tour of England in 1843, Cook, like many in the temperance movement, wrote to the churchman imploring him to visit the area, but for whatever reason, Mathew was not able to comply with Cook's request.

Cook now aimed to move beyond day trips to longer ventures and the first of these took place in the summer of 1845, when he organised a trip to Liverpool. This was a far more ambitious project than anything he had previously attempted and he prepared with great thoroughness. He did background research by visiting the town and staying in Brown's Temperance Hotel.

Walking the streets whilst in the town and taking in the sights and sounds, Cook began compiling what is now considered the first ever holiday brochure, *A Handbook of the Trip to Liverpool*. It directs travellers to visit such locations as the Canning and Salthouse Docks, police stations and the Mechanics Institute. The brochure informed visitors where to gain the best views of the town at that time at St. James' Mount (now the site of the Anglican Cathedral). He wrote of the location:

> *'There are very pleasing views. Indeed, the whole view is panoramic and picturesque and, when seen in the light of a midsummer morning before the smoke has arisen, the prospect is most charming.'*

Cook was certainly selling the town.

He also advised travellers to take a sea journey by steamship from Liverpool to Llandudno, absorb the Welsh scenery and spend a night in the town. Cook's first class passengers paid 15 shillings each and second-class ten shillings for the three-day excursion, with those who wanted to visit Wales paying a supplementary charge. The tour was a success and more trips to Liverpool followed. By the end of the decade Cook went on to establish further tours around Britain and then into Europe.

3. The Economic Divide: Poverty, Wealth, Leisure and Charity

Mid nineteenth century Liverpool was a place of diverse wealth. In a comparatively small town in size with an expanding population, the poor lived *'cheek by jowl'* with the wealthy. A couple of minutes' walk could take one from relatively luxurious surroundings to the poorest hovels. Moreover' it was not necessarily unemployment which drove many Liverpool citizens into poverty; lack of full-time and permanent work reduced many to a life of struggle.

For the middle and upper classes, though, with disposable income, life could be extremely enjoyable. There were material goods on which to spend their money, whilst there were an abundance of places of entertainment and other establishments in which to take pleasure. There were, however several affluent Liverpool citizens who believed their wealth should be applied to *'worthwhile causes'* and, therefore, charitable works dominated their lives.

Poverty

Poverty in 1840s Britain was a huge concern amongst, for example, novelists, observers and commentators. The novels of Charles Dickens are an obvious place to discover the nature of nineteenth century poverty, but others, such as Karl Marx's friend and co-author of the *Communist Manifesto* (1848), Frederick Engels, who spent a great deal of time researching the effects of poverty in his book *The Condition of the Working Class in England* (1842). 24-year-old Engels revealed the extent of the devastating effects of poverty on the working class of Manchester.

Another observer of the misery inflicted by poverty was Londoner, Henry Mayhew. A journalist, author, and playwright he was responsible for shining a light on the lives and living conditions of those at the margins of society. Mayhew was influenced by the deadly impact of cholera on London. Following the deaths of some 13,000 Londoners during the second major outbreak in 1849, he wrote an article detailing the effects of the disease on Bermondsey, an impoverished area of London.

Mayhew became more involved in a broader survey of the condition of the poorer classes and produced a series of newspaper articles published later that year. For the first time, the realities of days spent struggling to make a living on the streets of London followed by nights spent by many sleeping in its cheapest, dirtiest boarding houses were set out in great detail. His collected articles on poverty were eventually published as *London Labour and London Poor* (1851).

Another approach to the nature of poverty, this time in Liverpool, was provided by *Moby Dick* author, Herman Melville, in his semi-autobiographical novel *Redburn: His First Journey* (1849). Melville wrote of much of the *'wonders'* of the town, but also of the misery he saw whilst walking the streets of Liverpool. A New York sailor, Melville docked in the town on a few occasions and recorded many of the sights he encountered.

In one section of the novel Redburn is walking along Lancelot Hey, close to the docks, when he hears groaning emanating from a cellar. He discovers a woman and two children lying on a dirt floor. *'They were...next to dead with want. There they had crawled to die,'* he wrote. Redburn leaves the cellar to try to get assistance. Here he learns that the family have been in the cellar for three days and had had nothing to eat. He also learned that the family received little sympathy from those who knew them. One woman, rummaging for scraps through bins, told Redburn that the mother *'deserved to die'*, because she had never been married. Redburn then meets a policeman who tells him to return to his ship and not concern himself with such matters.

He eventually returns to his lodging house to collect food and water and returns to the cellar. He distributes the food and drink, which the children consume ravenously, but their mother *'refused to speak, eat or drink.'* Redburn then notices something underneath the woman's shawl and, lifting it, discovers the dead body of a baby. He revisited Lancelot Hey over the next two days and the family were still present. When he visited on the third day, however, the cellar was empty. Redburn only discovered:

> *'...a heap of quick-lime glistening. I could not learn who had taken them away, or whither they had gone; but my prayer was answered – they were dead, departed and at peace.'*

Redburn's discovery in the Lancelot Hey cellar was not unusual in 1840s Liverpool, such was the endemic nature of poverty in the town.

Poverty and its Consequences

On Wednesday 23 December 1846, mother of seven, Sarah Burns, was discovered dead in her bed in Thomas Street (off Paradise Street). When reported, the cause of her death shocked Liverpool as people were not supposed to die in such a manner in Victorian Britain. At her subsequent inquest, before Borough Coroner, Philip Finch Curry, the cause of death was recorded as starvation. Sarah had not eaten for the three days prior to her passing. Finch Curry heard that the family spent most of its time begging on the streets to survive.

Sarah Burns' death should not have occurred as the government had, in 1834, introduced a new Poor Law, which was partly devised to prevent such fatalities. Supporters welcomed the law because they believed it would, for example, take beggars (such as the Burns family) off the streets. Before 1834, the cost of looking after the poor was growing more expensive each year. This cost was paid for through the rates by the middle and upper classes in each town. There was a real suspicion amongst the ratepayers that they were funding an idle, indolent group of people, disinclined to work.

After years of complaint, a new Poor Law was introduced in 1834. The new law was intended to reduce the cost of looking after the poor and impose a system which would be identical across the country. Parishes were grouped into unions and, if they did not already have one, each union had to build a workhouse.

Liverpool did not immediately operate the new Poor Law. It was not until 25 March 1841 that Liverpool Poor Law Parish finally came into existence, originally under a 21-strong Board of Guardians elected by ratepayers, which the following year reverted to what was known as a Select Vestry with a board of 29 members. Liverpool's population, recorded in 1831 at 165,000, made it the largest parish in England. Except in special circumstances the poor could now only get help if they were prepared to leave home and go into a workhouse.

The Liverpool Select Vestry had responsibility for the operation of the Brownlow Hill Workhouse (now the site of Liverpool Metropolitan Cathedral) and its day-to-day management was supervised by a workhouse governor. Conditions inside workhouses were deliberately harsh, so that only those who desperately needed help would ask the parish for it. Inside the workhouse families were split up and housed in different parts of the institution. The inmates, as they were called, were made to wear uniforms and their diet was monotonous.

There were also strict rules and regulations to follow. Inmates, male and female, young and old were made to work hard, often doing unpleasant jobs such as picking oakum or breaking stones. Children could also find themselves hired out to work in factories, mines or, usually in Liverpool, domestic service. However, not all Victorians shared this point of view. Some people, such as Tory factory owner, Richard Oastler, spoke out against the new Poor Law, calling the workhouses *'Prisons for the Poor'*. Many people living in poverty hated and feared the threat of the workhouse so much that there were riots in some northern towns, such as at Todmorden in Yorkshire in 1838, where the homes of members of the Board of Guardians were attacked.

The workhouse therefore existed to prevent the deaths of people like Sarah Burns, so the middle and upper classes of Liverpool were, thus shocked when they read of her death. Why were people starving when a system existed to prevent such occurrences? Starvation though did occur and continued to do so in Liverpool following the death of Sarah Burns.

Within a few weeks, Finch Curry was hearing similar cases to that of Sarah Burns. The *Liverpool Mercury* of 8 January 1847 reported on the death of 16-year-old Patrick Curran on 30 December 1846. The inquest heard from his father Dennis who told the court that his family of eight had arrived from Ireland the previous Christmas Eve with eight shillings between them. After finding a house in Ashton Street they had just three shillings remaining, which they had to use to spend on what little food they could afford. On the 30th Dennis was awoken by the screams of his wife who had discovered Patrick dead in his bed. He told Finch Curry that he had never applied to the parish for relief. Surgeon Richard Hannon carried out the post-mortem and concluded that Patrick had died of starvation. He told the court that *'the stomach and intestines were perfectly empty ...I never saw so clear a case from dying from want of food.'* Finch Curry returned a verdict of *'death due to starvation.'* Patrick was buried in an unmarked pauper's grave in St Mary's Cemetery.

In an additional report in the same edition from the Coroner's Court, under the headline *'Another Death from Starvation'* the *Mercury* informed its readers of the passing of *'an infant, Mary Brady.'* Living in a *'wretched hole in Lace Street'* (off Vauxhall Road), the family of six would have all died had it not been for the intervention of Parish Relieving Officers who supplied them *'with temporary relief in the shape of soup and bread.'* The family clearly had not applied for parish relief, but the paper noticeably quoted Finch Curry stating the *'parish was acquitted of all blame.'*

On 8 May, eight-year-old Luke Brothers died of starvation. Finch Curry had taken the inquest jury to inspect the Brothers' family home on Banastre Street (off Vauxhall Road). In his address to the court he urged the press and the Select Vestry to visit the Brothers' home to see for themselves the *'...dreadful living conditions endured by many.'* The coroner said that deaths from diseases were horrific enough, but death from starvation was preventable. The Select Vestry employed relieving officers to visits homes. Finch Curry declared that:

> *'...if one relieving officer could not do the work then two ought to be employed ... if not, then twenty... if not, then forty.'*

Finch Curry was arguing not for the end of the Poor Law but for an examination of its shortcomings and its system of administration to prevent such deaths.

Within a few months it would appear that Finch Curry had travelled from his position of absolving the Parish of blame, as in the case of Mary Brady in January, to accusing the institution of not performing its duties adequately enough to prevent deaths. The Poor Law, and by extension the workhouses, were well established, but there were massive failures with its operation. What was so wrong that many families were seemingly prepared to face the prospect of imminent death rather than enter the workhouse?

Liverpool Workhouse

Within a few months of their establishment, several scandals involving the behaviour of workhouse staff hit the headlines. The most infamous was in Hampshire at the Andover Workhouse, where it was reported that: '*half-starved inmates were found eating rotting flesh from bones.*' In response to these scandals the government introduced stricter rules for those who ran the workhouses and they also set up a system of regular inspections. However, inmates were still at the mercy of governors who, opponents of the workhouse believed, treated the poor with contempt and abused rules.

Liverpool's Brownlow Hill workhouse was, at a cost of £25,000, rebuilt and enlarged in 1842, becoming one of the largest in the country with an official capacity of 1,800, but at times accommodating as many as 3,000. Like all workhouses, Liverpool adhered to government rules and a couple of brief examples of those rules help indicate why Richard Oastler referred to them as '*prisons *for the poor.'* For instance, with respect to work, the government declared that, *'The period for all paupers to work is from four in the morning to ten at night with three hours allowed for clearing away and sweeping the workhouse yard.'* For breaking workhouse rules, punishment could be very harsh. For instance:

> *'For being longer than ten minutes to each of the two meals per day, breakfast and supper, 39 lashes; for going out of the workhouse yard without permission, a day without food; for being disobedient 29 lashes and three days' confinement underground.'*

These regulations were swiftly enforced. For example, on 15 September 1842 four men and a boy were gaoled for 21 days for refusing to eat the porridge because it was *'not thick enough'*. Edward Rushton, the stipendiary magistrate, pronounced it *'the finest food ever given to a human being.'* Rushton continued to jail male and female inmates on a regular basis for offences such insubordination, disorderly conduct and assaulting staff.

Life had not begun well for the new workhouse. In February 1843, the Select Vestry met to consider some of the extraordinary statements regularly appearing in the local and national press, mainly as a result of a statement of Rushton's in which he described the workhouse as *'The largest brothel in England.'*

Reported in the *Mercury* on 17 February, Workhouse Governor James Dowdall was asked whether he thought the workhouse was indeed the largest brothel in England. He said he did not know *'what size the largest brothel in England was, but I do know the Liverpool Workhouse brothel.'* He added that if anyone *'absented themselves from dinner, intercourse might take place'* without his knowledge.

Moreover, male paupers were getting over the iron railing which separated their ward from the females.

Dowdall freely admitted that he could not control events, saying he feared going to the workhouse at night. An elderly female member of staff also told the meeting that she was unable to control the behaviour of the 30-40 girls in her charge. The Select Vestry declared that Governor Dowdall's *'health was broken and his mind injured'* and declared it was in everyone's best interest if he was relieved of his duties.

In agreement with Rushton, the meeting vowed to replace many existing staff members with younger, fitter employees and, as the re-building work was still in progress, to make it more difficult for outsiders to freely enter the workhouse by constructing perimeter walls higher with railings atop. The building work was completed and staffing changes introduced with Dowdall replaced as governor by Robert Evans in June 1843.

Six years later in December 1849, a journalist from the *Liverpool Journal* toured the Workhouse and on the 8th, reported his findings to the newspaper's readership. At the time of his visit the institution housed 1880 inmates of whom there were 380 boys and 198 girls under the age of 15. The reporter visited first the nursery in which 80 youngsters were accommodated. Mothers were allowed to visit their children for just two hours per week. The reporter asked one of the children where her mother was and the child replied, *'In the workhouse, unaware of her own surroundings.'* The reporter added:

> *'Seeing so many pretty children and knowing how proud the childless rich would be of such treasures, I asked if they had not now and then had some visitors enquiring about adopting.*

> *"Very rarely"* was the reply, *"but a lady not long ago chose a very fine boy and went off to live in Australia".'*

Next on the visit was a ward named *'The Class'* which was reserved for *'mothers of illegitimate children and prostitutes.'* There were 110 inmates here employed in oakum picking, washing linen or grinding corn for which each woman was required to grind 47 pounds per day. The matron of the ward told the reporter that the women *'did not view this work or the oakum picking as hard work.'*

The reporter ventured next to the male workrooms, where the men were employed as blacksmiths, cobblers, tailors and coffin makers. Here he met an *'old man'* named as Patrick Moran who said that in his youth he had *'been a soldier in the British Army'* who had *'fought against the French'* (presumably during the Napoleonic Wars). The reporter was impressed by the work and efforts of the men. He concluded his tour of the main workhouse by saying that he believed the institution overall was very impressive. Likening the workhouse to a machine he stated *'the mechanism of which is all that could be desired.'*

During the typhus epidemic of 1847 the council built *'fever sheds'* on the junction of Mount Pleasant and Brownlow Hill to accommodate many victims of the disease. In March 1848, the sheds, now part of the workhouse complex, were re-used as a *'night asylum for houseless poor'*. The first Liverpool night asylum was established in Freemasons Row, Vauxhall in 1830 with another opening later in Soho Street, Everton. The asylums were charitable institutions designed to take the homeless off the streets.

Entering asylums was not always easy, particular during the Irish Famine year of 1847. Nancy Dougherty and her daughter had tried to enter the Soho Street asylum on the evening of 5 June 1847 but they could not get in. Nancy lying in a nearby passage was found dead the following morning. A police officer told her inquest, reported in the *Liverpool* Chronicle on the 12th, *'I found a group of wretched people lying there and in their midst, I found the dead woman.*

The *Journal's* reporter made the Brownlow Hill Night Asylum the final location of his tour of the workhouse complex. On the night of his visit he found 97 males and 67 females in residence. The accommodation was intended for those who could not afford lodgings, so upon entering the lodgers they were first stripped and searched to ensure they were penniless because if any money was found on their person they would be taken to prison overnight, placed before the magistrate the following morning, charged with deception and possibly jailed if found guilty.

The lodgers slept on bare boards overnight and were woken at six in the morning. Their accommodation, however, was not obtained gratis. When awoken, they were immediately set to work for four hours picking oakum. The doors of the asylum were opened at ten and the lodgers sent back on to the Liverpool streets.

The reporter spoke to some of the asylum's inmates whom he said were: *'apart from the odd vagrant, all beggars, prostitutes and thieves.'* Yet his interviews are almost all with children of whom he said the youngest was *'merely a girl of seven,'* whilst another was a girl of twelve who described herself as *'a prostitute.'* He spoke to nine-year-old Hugh Lavery, once of Circus Street, near Islington, who said his father and brother had deserted him and for the past three weeks he had lived on the streets surviving as a pickpocket. He mainly stole silk handkerchiefs which he then sold for *'two or three pennies in Fontenoy Street, near Tithebarn Street.*

The reporter's conclusion, *'the asylum should be shut down'* and the applicants left to fend for themselves. He wrote:

> *'...while the foxes of the earth have holes, the very destitute should not have some half-comfortable shelter provided for them.'*

The system was open to abuse and should end, he added. His final statement: *'The true vagrant's home is the bridewell and the sooner the authorities realise this the better.'* There was no condemnation from him, for example, of a society that allows *'a client'* to sexually abuse a twelve-year-old girl on the streets of Liverpool.

The Working Poor

Poverty was not the sole proviso of the unemployed; a significant number of those in work also suffered its debilitating effects. In 1842, John Finch (the alcohol abstinence campaigner) of the Liverpool Anti-Monopoly Association conducted a survey to inform the Liverpool public regarding the devastating consequences of poverty. Entitled *'Statistics of Vauxhall Ward Liverpool showing the actual condition of more than 5,000 families',* the report made several revelatory discoveries of which the *Liverpool Journal* of 16 April 1842 said the town should be *'embarrassed by the magnitude of distress.'* Of the 5,000 families Finch ascertained that there were:

> 1737 unemployed
> 1587 partially employed
> 1490 fully employed

He further described half of the homes as *'comfortable or tolerable'*; with the other half described as *'bad, miserable or destitute'*. Finch calculated that a family of four needed to earn £1 (labour value in 2016 about £500) per week to live in relative comfort. His report though showed that just 543 families grossed this amount, so the great majority, including many in employment, struggled to survive week-to-week.

What made the struggle much harder for Finch, and the *raison d'être* for his report, was the price of food and in particular, bread. He determined that bread alone accounted for a third of the expenditure of most of the families earning less than £1 per week. He claimed that this compared dramatically to prices in 1835 when the cost of bread accounted for around one fifth of a similar family's budget.

Finch, who as an iron merchant and employer said he would not pay his workers less than three shillings per day, received correspondence from shopkeepers and bakers who too complained about the price of bread. Their letters reveal plummeting sales of bread as many people could not afford to buy from them and they were instead buying cheaper, inferior produce. In conclusion, Finch stressed his report was not an appeal to charity to come to the aid of the poor, but an appeal to the government to control the food monopolies who were fixing prices for their own profits at the expense of the poor.

In his report, Finch categorised the industries in which people were employed. In a ward, such as Vauxhall, which included most of the north docks, it was no surprise that it was shipping which topped the table of employment; approximately one third of people worked in some capacity in that industry. A large proportion of those, however, would have been in the temporary employment category as dock labourers or porters.

Trying to find work on the docks at the time was a demonstration of struggle and endurance for many. Casualism was the order of the day meaning dock workers and warehouse porters (known as Operative Porters) could only find work, for example, for just a few hours per day and sometimes no more than a couple of days a week.

According to the local guidebook *'A Stranger's Guide to Liverpool'* (1846), casualism was a highly-approved system of employment. *'It was a symbol of independence',* the best guarantee of *'freedom from work-discipline'* and from the tyranny of the factory bell. The evidence though suggests that, amongst the porters at least, this interpretation of casualism was not one they recognised. For them casualism was not so much a symbol of independence but a symbol of poverty.

In March 1848, the porters demonstrated against the system outside the Town Hall. They were attempting to persuade ship owners and merchants to change the arrangements of their employment known as *'master porterage.'* The master porters were middlemen who hired warehouse porters on behalf of the merchants. This gave them total power over hiring, as well as giving them the power to determine the length of a day's work and pay. In addition to these constraints, many of the porters were paid regularly in local pubs, of which the master porters usually held an interest, at the end of a working day; the paymaster was usually surrounded by *'bullies.'*

The porters produced a poster (which can be seen online at the National Archives) to coincide with the demonstrations. It was headlined to *'The Merchants and Brokers of Liverpool'* and it made appeals to them to abolish the system. Calling themselves *'The Warehouse Porters of Liverpool'* they said they had *'spent the winter in privation'* deprived of work because of the type of workers hired by the master porters instead of them. They claimed the master porters *'engaged men who were careless and wasteful'* with the merchandise costing the owners money; also *'drunkards'* were employed in preference to sober men; finally, they claimed single men were often preferred to married men who had the more urgent need for work. Although Chief Magistrate Edward Rushton appeared sympathetic to their cause, for example he pledged to abolish the system whereby workers were paid in the pub; he did suggest they petition parliament and not the town council. The men continued to protest daily until they were finally cleared by a police baton charge.

The porters and dockers' plight was highlighted to the public of Liverpool on 1 December 1849. The *Liverpool Journal* reported on the difficulties faced by the casually employed workers in their search for employment and the ensuing problems they encountered when employed on short time or facing extended periods of unemployment.

The *Journal* claimed that there were about 17,000 men working at the port, either loading and unloading ships or working in the warehouses. It added that the maximum a docker or porter could earn was three shillings and sixpence per day (a day's work being twelve hours), thus earning about £1 per week. Broadly agreeing with Finch's conclusions on adequate levels of pay, the paper stated, *'This income would allow the labourer and his family to live in comparative comfort.'* In an obvious rejoinder, it did though add that labourers were only likely to work for about two days per week, resulting in a life of struggle.

To find employment, workers had to gather daily at Exchange Flags at the rear of the Town Hall and wait to be selected for work. Dock foremen and master porters' representatives would arrive early in the morning to choose the required number of workers for a day's or sometimes half a day's labour. The *Journal's* unnamed reporter spoke to some of the men including Charles Cassidy of Bent Street, described as an *'elderly man'* who had worked at the docks for thirty years. Cassidy told the reporter that he had not had one day's work in the last seven weeks. James Lorimer another *'elderly man'* said he had *'not worked for a long time and was often ashamed to go home.'* Finally, Thomas Smith, a man who had worked as a labourer on and off for over forty years, had worked two and a half days in the previous ten weeks.

The interviewees also informed the paper that when they did find work they were rarely paid the full rate of three shillings and sixpence. Of 100 or so men interviewed the reporter learned that just five had been paid the full rate for their last full day's work. Many had been paid three shillings and some as little as two shillings. The men also claimed that sometimes young boys were employed and paid just one shilling and sixpence for a day's labour.

Complaining about pay was difficult, said several men, due to two factors; first, a complaint meant the men were unlikely to be hired again; second, the men felt intimidated by the *'bullies'* when picking up their wages in the local pub. They were forced to accept their lot, owing to the threats of violence.

The porters referred to the method of hiring as *'corrupt, unjust and evil,'* which was injurious to the merchants as well as porters. The appeal though fell on deaf ears. As the *Journal's* report shows almost two years after the protests at the town hall, the system was still in place. The reporter stated that every porter he had spoken to condemned the arrangements. He called both the method of hiring workers and payment of wages in the manner used by the master porters as *'petty terrorism.'* The Dock Labourers Union was aiming to tackle both the system of casualisation and pay he wrote. In 1849 two associations of dock workers had been formed; the Liverpool South End Dockers and the Liverpool Operative Porters.

The reporter moved on to ask the men how they coped with so little, infrequent income. One anonymously informed him that:

> *'some will not earn more than £1 in seven weeks. Some of them have credit at the shops. The wives of some of the men take in washing. Some strive to live on one meal per day. I have not earned £3 in the last three months.'*

Another man said he earned nine shillings per week and when asked how he his wife and three children managed to survive he replied:

> *'We only strive to live. We have trust at the local shop, but if we cannot pay the bill on a Saturday night we have no more credit.'*

The reporter added that the family had pawned most of its possessions. There was an interesting gap in the report; there were no references whatsoever to applications to the parish for support. It would be fair to assume that the great majority of those interviewed must have been prepared to take their chances on the outside than face the demoralising prospect of life in the workhouse.

Dockers and porters continued to survive *'hand to mouth'* for the remainder of the nineteenth century as casualism persisted on the docks into the following century. It was one factor in the huge transport strike which involved thousands of workers in the summer of 1911. However, it took almost one hundred years from the reports of 1849 to effectively end the system when the British government created the National Dock Labour Board in 1947. The scheme was administered by the national and local boards, made up of equal numbers of persons representing dock workers. Each local board was responsible for keeping a register of employers and workers, paying wages and attendance money, controlling the hiring of labour, and had responsibility for discipline. The government abolished the scheme in 1989.

Prosperous Liverpool

There was a huge increase in the income and wealth of Liverpool based merchants and businessmen involved in shipping and associated commercial activities such as commodity exchanges, banking and insurance. Many of these firms constructed elegant office buildings around the Pier Head and Castle Street. So great was the wealth generated by such industries that the Bank of England opened its first ever branch outside London on Castle Street in 1848.

An array of material and personal goods was available to those in possession of a relatively well paid job or in ownership of a respectable amount of individual wealth. Dedicated solely to advertisements, the front pages of all Liverpool newspapers informed and persuaded its better off readers to part with their money to advance their social standing or improve their personal well-being. Newspapers carried adverts for goldsmiths, silversmiths and jewellers on Lord Street, where, in the latter, tiaras, necklaces and other expensive accessories could be purchased. In Bold Street and Castle Street, numerous tailors, dressmakers, hatters and milliners advertised their wares. Alcohol, wine and spirits of all kind could be bought by the dozen. Opticians publicised their range of spectacles and monocles, whilst for those concerned about the state of their teeth, there were dentists to tend to their problems.

Several of those at the higher end of the wealth and income scale desired more extravagant lifestyles. A select few, including many of the town's leading businessmen and gentry such as Lord Sandon, established the Mersey Yacht Club on 26 July 1844. In September, Prime Minister, Robert Peel enrolled as a member. On 23 September Queen Victoria granted it royal status and the club still carries that name today. By September, ten ships had registered with the club and they all sailed together on the Mersey for the first time that month.

The Roscoe Club, another institution for the preserve of the wealthy, was founded as an outcome of a public meeting held on 22 April 1847. A petition of the wealthier inhabitants of Liverpool to the Mayor, Thomas Berry Horsfall, requested such a meeting as several preliminary meetings had already been held as the result of a series of letters to the *Liverpool Weekly News.*

The Roscoe Club eventually opened in Clayton Square on 1 October for a:
> '...large body of young men engaged in businesses. It was established to '...encourage mental contribution and introduce a taste for the fine arts.'

The club's facilities included a dining room, coffee room, reading and news room, a library and reference room, a gymnasium and baths. Ten guineas was the price of a life membership with a further 25 shillings' annual subscription.

On 12 October, a letter from A. Porter (it's not clear whether that was the writer's name or job title) appeared in the *Mercury* protesting about the '...*monopolisation of such institutions by the middle classes.*' He added that:

> '...*the poor man naturally shrinks from coming into contact with those who appropriate to themselves superiority in intellect and wealth.*'

Porter called for: '...*an establishment of an institution for the working man to aid moral and mental advancement.*'

The author's concerns over the supremacy of the Roscoe Club would have, as it happened, not have lasted long. By September 1850, the Club's expenditure exceeded its income; bills such as those to builders went unpaid and its activities had to be suspended. The club initially closed temporarily, but it never re-opened.

Liverpool Zoo

Opened to the public in West Derby Road on 27 May 1833, the Liverpool Zoological Gardens (or Zoo) was located in an area which is today bounded by West Derby Road, Lowhill and Kensington, moving on out towards Shiel Road. It held animals from all over the world including lions, tigers, leopards, hyenas, pumas, jackals and sloths, as well as many birds such as penguins, macaws and parrots.

The zoo's prized attraction though was a huge Indian elephant named Rajah. Rajah had been purchased in India 1837 at a cost of £800. Looked after and ridden by head elephant keeper, Richard Howard and his assistant Henry Andrews, Rajah would, daily, tow visitors around the gardens in a cart. In the 1840s entrance to the zoo and gardens cost one shilling and attendees were given a token bearing the image of Rajah.

As its name indicates, the zoo not only held an international collection of animals but was designed for leisurely walks. The 1834 *Liverpool Stranger's Guide* described it thus. The gardens:

> '...have been laid out with walks and grass plots and the plants and the shrubs, which have been tastefully arranged, are in a healthy condition and promise to make this one of the most agreeable promenades in the vicinity.'

Looking down on the town below with its smoke and fumes, the gardens would have made a welcome break for Liverpool's middle class. Illustrations of the gardens at the time depict well dressed families strolling through enjoying the surroundings.

The owner, Thomas Atkins, was formerly a proprietor of a menagerie which travelled the country. The opening of the Liverpool to Manchester Railway in 1830, however, changed life for Atkins. Instead of him taking his collection of animals to the people, the people could now come to visit them. The railway meant Atkins could now attract not just Liverpolitans but the middle class from other parts of Lancashire too. The zoo was but a few minutes' walk from Liverpool's first railway station at Crown Street.

On 1 December 1843, assistant elephant keeper, Henry Andrews, was found dead in Rajah's cage. At the subsequent inquest, the details of which were printed in the *Liverpool Mercury* on 5 December, the coroner Philip Finch Curry heard that Andrews died as a consequence of massive internal injuries.

A broken broomstick was found in the cage. Witnesses including Andrews' co-workers said it was common for the assistant to hit Rajah with the broom. They told Finch Curry that they believed that the elephant may well have responded violently to one of these beatings and turned on the keeper. As there were no witnesses to the actual incident, the coroner felt he could not confidently agree with them and the jury, following the Finch Curry's recommendation, returned a verdict of accidental death. The *Mercury* reported that Thomas Atkins considered destroying Rajah but without the firm evidence of the creature's actions he was disinclined to do so. Rajah in any case was the main attraction.

On Saturday 17 June 1848 two visitors, Mr and Mrs Liversedge, made the railway trip from their Stockport home to visit the zoo enticed by the prospect of seeing a live elephant for the first time ever, but their experience that day was not one they desired.

On that morning, the couple were in the elephant house observing headkeeper Richard Howard cleaning one part of Rajah's cage with a broom before moving on to another part where the elephant was standing. The Liversedges watched on as Howard encouraged the elephant to move. Rajah refused to do so and Howard hit the elephant across his trunk with the broom. Rajah reacted by pushing Howard against the bars of the cage with *'great force.'* Howard fell to the floor and *'the elephant then stood on him with tremendous force.'* The Liversedges ran to raise the alarm. Zoo staff members soon arrived and pulled Howard from the cage. He had though died almost instantaneously.

Proprietor Thomas Atkins died a couple of days before the incident, so Rajah's future was now the responsibility of his eldest son, John.

The events which followed were reported in the *Mercury*. The paper reported that John Atkins spoke to his mother and they immediately took the decision to have the animal destroyed. The question was, how to accomplish this unsavoury act. At first, uncertain how to proceed, Atkins, having decided how to act, contacted Head Constable Dowling and Stipendiary Magistrate, Edward Rushton and asked permission to borrow a cannon from the Albert Dock. He also requested a contingent of soldiers from a nearby army barracks. Armed with rifles about 30 men duly arrived at the zoo.

While events were developing, three doctors named O'Donnell, Owen and Copper, arrived at the elephant house. Rather than destroying Rajah by a violent act, such as cannon or rifle fire, the doctors recommended a different solution. They recommended a poisonous substance, combining prussic acid, aconite and treacle, be administered in a bun. The *Mercury* takes up the story:

> 'In about five minutes after he had taken the poison he sank to his knees, lay down on his side, but in a few minutes, he recovered himself, rose and walked about in his ordinary, healthy state.'

Stunned observers stood watching and waiting for the poison to take effect, but after about 45 minutes the doctors determined Rajah had not been fatally harmed. Thankfully, John Atkins was disinclined to use the cannon, but instead turned to the soldiers. Twelve of them aimed and all hit Rajah. The elephant somehow managed to survive the volley of bullets. A second set of soldiers moved forward and fired, this time fatally wounding Rajah, who fell to the floor and died shortly afterwards.

News of the dramatic events spread rapidly and hundreds of people attempted to enter the zoo. Despite the Atkins family ordering the gates to be locked, many people managed to gain entry and some witnessed the unedifying spectacle. In a strange aside, the *Mercury* believed Thomas Atkins had missed an opportunity to make a substantial profit that day. In the days proceeding, he made amends for the oversight as advertisements appeared in the local press persuading people to come and see the body of Rajah in his cage, where he was left to lie for five days. Thousands of people did so.

Mr Liversedge's evidence, detailed above, was given at the coroner's inquest into Howard's death on 17 June and reported in the *Liverpool Courier* on the 25 June. Following Mr. Liversedge in the witness box was one of the zoo's gardeners, Thomas Lloyd, who said he had confronted Howard on the Friday evening before his death. Lloyd told the court that Rajah, with the headkeeper in charge, had been towing a party of visitors around the gardens when Howard began whipping the elephant. Lloyd protesting, asked him to stop. This was not the first time that Howard had behaved in this manner, he regularly beat the elephant, the gardener said. He further added that he believed the animal was not a threat to the public. Coroner Finch Curry agreed.

Finch Curry, whose anger is clear in his reported words, believed Rajah should not have been destroyed because the elephant *'was retaliating to acts of violence.'* He told the court that he had been informed that some of the people who had arrived at the zoo that day were prepared to buy the elephant from the Atkins family, but it had declined the offer. The coroner advised the jury that, unlike the death of Andrews five years earlier, Howard's demise was not accidental. The jury returned the following verdict:

'We are of the opinion that the deceased came by his death as a consequence of beating the elephant unmercifully thus causing the animal in his fury to kill him.'

The Zoological Gardens continued to attract visitors but by the 1860s they went into something of a decline and eventually closed in 1867 as the town of Liverpool expanded into West Derby.

The Grand National

The world's most famous horse race run under its current soubriquet, the *Grand National Steeplechase,* was run at Aintree Racecourse in 1847. From 1836 to 1838, a similar race took place at nearby Maghull, the first of which was won by The Duke ridden by Captain Martin Becher. Called the *Grand Liverpool Steeplechase*, the official history of the *Grand National* discounts these first three races. It is not until 1839 when the race transfers to Aintree and is titled the *Liverpool and National Steeplechase*, that it is officially recognised. During the first official race in 1839, Captain Becher famously fell from his horse and landed in a brook running under a fence which now bears his name.

The advent of the railways, spread the popularity of the steeplechase far and wide and it quickly became a great attraction in the sporting and social calendar. Contemporary newspapers wrote of carriages bringing wealthier citizens to the course, whilst thousands of the less well-off walked the four miles or so from the town centre, *'tramping up Scotland Road, through the fields of Kirkdale'* on their way to Aintree. During the decade, newspapers often wrote of the race meeting being *'an excuse for people to partake in drunken revelries.'*

The 1840 race received a great deal of criticism for the dangers it posed to both horse and rider. Run on 5 March, and reported in the *Mercury* on the 6th, the fence in front of the stands, a stone wall, caused particular consternation. Lottery, winner in 1839, reached the obstacle in second place before falling *'amid a flurry of dismantled masonry.'* Three horses were brought down and one rider, Tom Olliver, lay motionless for some time. Suffering concussion and a broken collar bone, he was eventually taken to the safety of the stands. *'Olliver's condition led some spectators to believe he had been killed.'* The race was eventually won by Jerry, ridden by local jockey Bartholomew Bretherton at a price of 16/1.

The *Mercury* was outraged by the use of a stone wall as a fence. Defenders of the obstacle said it represented a natural feature of the countryside where many horses trained. The *Mercury* and other critics got their way the following year when the wall was replaced with a water jump, 15 feet wide and three feet deep. Tom Olliver, meanwhile, recovered sufficiently to ride consecutive winners in 1842 and 1843. Although he finished placed on a couple of more occasions, riding in a total of 15 nationals, Olliver never managed to win another National.

The race was renamed the now famous *'Grand National Steeplechase'* for the first time in 1847. Taking place on 3 March the *Liverpool Mail* reported that, *'a huge crowd of people, high and low, rich and poor flocked to the course.'* The race attracted a then record field of 26 runners, only seven of whom completed the arduous course.

Coincidentally, the race was won by a horse called Mathew, named after the *'Apostle of Temperance'*, Father Theobald Mathew, which was owned by a controversial Irish landowner, John Courtney. The 1847 race took place in the year of the disastrous Great Famine of Ireland (see Chapter Five) when tens of thousands of starving Irish fled their homeland and arrived in Liverpool. It is likely that several of the fleeing Irish may well have worked on Courtney's Cork estate, as he had forcibly and controversially evicted 114 tenant potato farmers for a failure to pay rent.

In 1849, Peter Simple, a horse ridden and trained by Tom Cunningham, won the final race of the decade, but this was another contest mired in controversy. The race starter, Lord Sefton, across whose land it was run, declared a false start. Reports later suggested that, owing to the noise of a raucous crowd, the jockeys failed to hear Sefton's cries for a recall and the race continued. Despite the false start, the result stood.

The controversy arose as a consequence of the deaths of three horses. The three runners had all fallen at the third fence. While one horse got up and attempted to run off, two horses, so badly injured, were still on the track when the field jumped the fence again on the second circuit, causing others to fall. The three badly injured horses were destroyed after the race. Papers again called for the fences to be modified, which did not immediately happen. Despite the tragedies, the Grand National went on to become one of the major events in Liverpool's sporting and social calendar.

Theatre-going

Theatre-going, like horse racing, was not the total preserve of the middle and upper classes. Theatre owners required audiences drawn from all social classes and to attract members of the working class in the 1840s, some venues charged as little as three old pennies for a gallery seat. Attending the theatre or music hall was extremely popular in Liverpool and no more so than when some of the world's most famous shows, entertainers, actors or actresses came to town.

One such American entertainer Charles Sherwood Stratton arrived in the winter of 1844 aboard the Cunard steamship *Cambria*. Stratton was part of the famous Phineas Taylor (P.T.) Barnum's show which embarked on a UK countrywide tour that year. When Stratton was a child, showman Barnum, his distant cousin, was keen to include him in his cast of entertainers, hence he taught the boy to sing and dance. The motivation, however, behind Barnum's eagerness to integrate Stratton in his show was the boy's height.

Charles had stopped growing in his second year and remained at just two feet tall. Barnum bestowed the name *'General Tom Thumb'* upon the boy and he quickly became the star of his travelling show. He was put on a month's trial at Barnum's notorious American Museum in New York and had pride of place in the line-up. Barnum claimed that half a million Americans had seen Tom performing before he departed for Liverpool.

In February 1844 Tom Thumb, described by Barnum as *'The Smallest Person that ever Walked Alone'*, made his first ever British public appearance in Liverpool. Advertised on the front pages of all Liverpool newspapers, he was to appear for one week at two separate venues; beginning on Saturday 10 February, in the evening he was to perform, *'Depicting the Greek statues and Napoleon'*, at the *Theatre Royal*, Church Street, while during the day Barnum arranged for his prodigy to be *'exhibited'* in the Portico at number eight Newington, a narrow street connecting Bold Street and

Renshaw Street. To see Tom Thumb at the *Portico,* visitors were required to pay sixpence.

Reporting on Tom's appearances, the Liverpool press, though praiseworthy, was rather low key. The *Mercury* on 16 February, in a short review headlined '*Tom Thumb the Great*' wrote that he:

> '*Delighted crowds of young folk and adult friends. He sings Yankee Doodle Dandy like a child. He impersonates Napoleon and in various ways amuses his visitors in a manner likely to make him very popular.*'

A few lines in the *Liverpool Mail* on the 17th described Tom as '*...active, intelligent but somewhat childish in manner.*'

Following his Liverpool appearances, Tom Thumb set off for London. Appearing in the capital at the *Princess's Theatre*, his reputation quickly grew, so much so that he was invited to Buckingham Palace to meet Queen Victoria and other members of the royal family. Meeting the queen was a great coup for Barnum who used the event to advertise his shows on the subsequent UK tour.

On 23 August, Barnum's show returned to Liverpool to begin a six-day run of three two hour shows per day at the *Royal Liver Theatre*, Church Street, which could accommodate an audience of almost one thousand people. As a consequence of the publicity in meeting the queen and unlike his first appearance in the town, this was no low-key affair. The show and Tom Thumb in particular, was widely advertised on the front pages of all Liverpool newspapers. The advert stated that 300,000 people in Britain had witnessed the spectacle and went on to read:

> 'Tom Thumb is lively, interesting, intelligent and graceful in his manners and of the most symmetrical proportions. He will relate his history and represent Napoleon in full military costume. He will also appear in full court dress.'

All shows sold out and in its review the *Liverpool Albion* described Tom Thumb as a:

> '...funny little fellow who was a hit with the ladies who queued to kiss him. His imitation of Napoleon gives evidence of taste and faculties of a very high order.'

The paper also praised his singing which *'will give joy to all who have the opportunity to hear him.'* The *Albion* went on to explain how he walked through the auditorium, post show, selling his book and souvenirs.

The Liverpool public were undoubtedly captivated by Tom Thumb. Although not in usage at the time, he was certainly a mid-nineteenth century celebrity. In between shows, hundreds of people thronged his accommodation to catch a glimpse or obtain his autograph. So much was his popularity that he was soon presented around the town on top of a horse drawn cart. During one of the excursions, a cartwheel ran over the leg of a 15-year-old boy who was admitted to the Southern Hospital. Barnum received more publicity for his shows when he arranged for Tom to present the hospital with a £5 donation.

So much was his growing popularity that the *Mercury* on 27 September felt compelled to publish a lengthy poem in praise of Tom Thumb. The first four lines of which read:

All hail Tom Thumb of Lilliputian race
Thou art the gem of every glittering place
Precocious talent aids thy tiny form
To sing – to dance – or bygone scenes perform

On the same front page, a shop in the town centre advertised the sale for sixpence each: *'Full length miniature figures of Tom'*. Not everyone was however enamoured with the manifestation of the 'General.' One man writing to the *Liverpool Mail* on 27 August, complained about his wife's insistence on parting with one shilling to purchase his book:

> 'The little man was walking around calling "buy my book." My wife immediately asked me for one shilling. One hundred female hands went in the air holding a shilling each.'

The author added that the only thing his wife was interested in was the general's *'stamped receipt'* – a kiss. His wife, not carrying her own money, *'begged'* her husband for a shilling to buy the book and get her kiss. He gave her the shilling; she got her kiss and was extremely happy; he was most definitely not!

The public and the press were, though, a little deceived by Barnum and Tom Thumb. While the press and the public were describing him as a *'little fellow'* or *'little man,'* Tom was still a child. At the time of his visit to Liverpool, Barnum was telling the public that he was 13 years old. He was in fact just six years of age. No surprise therefore that the *Mercury* wrote of him as *'singing like a child'* with the *Mail* describing him as *'...somewhat childish in manner.'*

Charles Stratton was born on 4 January 1838 in Bridgeport, Connecticut. When Barnum met the Stratton family in 1842 he suggested to them that they tell the world he was English and eleven years old. Though initially disliking the idea the Strattons agreed to acquiesce with Barnum's plan. Charles' parents accompanied him on his tour of the UK. He was a massive success wherever he performed, as indeed he was in Liverpool. Such was the triumph of his return to the town, a further 21 performances over seven days were added to the calendar. All shows went on to sell out, resulting in around 40,000 people visiting the theatre.

Tom Thumb returned to Liverpool during the winter of 1846-47. Beginning a show on 11 December 1846 at the *New Theatre Royal, Adelphi* on Christian Street (off Islington), it was scheduled to run for one week. The show encompassed two acts; the first entitled *'Hop O' My Thumb'* in which the front-page adverts in all Liverpool newspapers read, *'Tom will be performing Scotch songs and dance the Highland Fling.'*

In the second act, the advert read, *'Tom represents the Greek statues including depictions of Hercules, Cupid and Ajax'*. As in 1844, there was great enthusiasm to catch a glimpse of the entertainer outside as well as inside the theatre. Staying at 110 Bold Street, his *'celebrity'* continued as his hotel was again besieged by fans and he also took to travelling around the town centre, this time in his purpose-built carriage, waving to adoring crowds. His appearances were again roaring successes and the show was extended to run until 2 January 1847. Evidently the Liverpool public could not get enough of the phenomenon that was Tom Thumb.

* *

Perhaps the most famous mid-nineteenth century actor was the renowned Shakespearian performer, Charles Kean (his father, Edmund, had been equally famous in his time) who performed at the

Theatre Royal Williamson Square in May 1844. His appearance, however, was not fully appreciated by all in attendance. Reviewing his performances in a 17th century play entitled *'The Gamester'*, the *Liverpool Mercury* on 17 May reported much consternation in the audience. The paper quoted Kean saying that he refused to play *'in front of a sixpenny gallery.'* Kean had, the *Mercury* said, insisted that prices should be doubled or else he would refuse to perform. The theatre obliged, but the audience let him know that they didn't approve. When he made his first appearance on the evening of the 13th, *'the audience hissed and booed and Kean stood there staring at them in stony silence.'*

There was further trouble the following evening. One man, Robert Knowles-Canter, booed Kean as he walked on, while another, Edward Moss, objected to Knowles-Canter's actions and rebuked him. Knowles-Canter responded by *'hitting Moss with his walking cane and kicking him down some stairs.'* The *Mercury* reported that the following day Knowles-Canter appeared at the magistrates' court charged with assault. He was convicted and fined £5.

In February of 1844 the *Theatre Royal* Williamson Square staged one of the first theatrical performances of Charles Dickens' *A Christmas Carol*. The *Liverpool Mail* reported that *'Mr Lambert's portrayal of Ebenezer Scrooge reduced many in the audience to tears.'* It added that other scenes from the play were greeted with *'great laughter …never had so many had such fun.'*

On Monday 5 June 1848, Dickens himself appeared as the character Shallow in Shakespeare's *The Merry Wives of Windsor* at the *Royal Amphitheatre*, Great Charlotte Street. Though only in a minor role, Dickens' appearance helped push up admission prices with the cheapest gallery seat, usually costing around one shilling, doubling in price and a private box for eight priced £4/4 shillings.

Dickens, well known for his readings at St. George's Hall from the mid-1850s onwards, did make appearances in Liverpool much earlier. For example, he was invited to address the Liverpool Mechanics Institute (later the Liverpool Institute and then LIPA). The institute, a mainly fee paying educational institution with day and evening schools, also housed a library holding over 11,000 books, and received magazines and periodicals from different parts of the country. Members paid a subscription of ten shillings and sixpence per year to use the service.

Originally invited to address the institution at Christmas 1842, Dickens was forced to cancel the event, which was re-arranged for 26 February 1844. Such was his reverence by the Liverpool public, the show was a sell- out with 1,200 visitors paying four shillings each to attend. The *Mercury* wrote of *'...carriages and coaches parked in all parts of the town including Mount Street, Rodney Street and Hope Street.'* Speakers were highly praiseworthy of Dickens and his work. In return he praised the aims of the institute and regaled his audience with tales of his life and experiences. His audience were keen to hear the stories that became the basis of his novels.

Classical Music and the Philharmonic Hall

The middle and upper classes of Liverpool greatly appreciated classical musical performances. For example, the famed Hungarian composer, Franz Liszt, performed to great acclaim at the *Theatre Royal*, Williamson Square on 1 December 1840. The *Playhouse Theatre* bears a blue plaque to commemorate Liszt and the event. On

10 January of the same year the Liverpool Philharmonic Society and Orchestra was established. It originally practised and performed in a hall in Great Richmond Street, Everton.

In 1843 the orchestra moved to the newly opened castle-like edifice of the Liverpool Collegiate in nearby Shaw Street, and performed to packed audiences. Opened by William Gladstone, the Collegiate was a fee-paying boys' school for wealthy Liverpool citizens. The orchestra performed *'full dress'* concerts at the venue and the third such event on 14 August 1843 attracted an audience of over 1,700. Enjoying the music of Rossini, Mozart and English and Italian opera, the *Mercury* reported on the 18th that, *'all the performances were greatly cheered.'*

The concert was though spoilt by heavy rain which could be heard on the roof as orchestra performed. The experience may well have played its part on subsequent events with regards to the Philharmonic's location. The *Mercury* was however more incensed concerning the aftermath of the concert owing to the chaotic organisation of carriages which were picking up members of the audience outside in the heavy rain. People had, the paper wrote:

> *'...the inconvenience of standing around in the hall for a prolonged and insufferable extent. The ladies had to be walked to their carriages in the arms of gentlemen who were wetted to the skin during their arduous and gallant services. There was as much discomfort as was ever witnessed on any public occasion. If only the stewards and the numerous body of police would have taken care to announce the carriages as they drove up to the door, regularity and despatch would have occurred. We earnestly advise that in the future this be implicitly regarded.'*

Such was the popularity of the orchestra, and perhaps the experience of the full-dress concert, there was great demand from the moneyed classes for a purpose-built concert hall. In 1844, the Philharmonic Society invited architect John Cunningham to prepare plans for a 2,100-seat concert hall to be constructed on Hope Street. To help cover some of the cost of the hall, members of the public were invited to purchase boxes designed for six people. The prices for these seats ranged from 80 to 110 guineas, (price value about £8,000 - £11,000 in 2016) a guinea being £1 and one shilling. Annual subscriptions also had to be paid by those purchasing boxes. Subscriptions were also taken for stall seats.

Work began and preparations were put in place for performances in the opening week. In early 1847 the society negotiated successfully with renowned German composer Felix Mendelssohn who agreed to perform at the opening concerts for a fee of £105 (wages value about £80,000 in 2016). Sadly, though, aged just 38, Mendelssohn died on 4 November 1847. The Philharmonic Concert Hall was completed in the spring of 1849 and the grand opening performance was set for 27 August. 65 boxes and 600 stall seats had been purchased, a figure below the society's expectations. *The Times* laid the responsibility for this firmly on the society's price of one guinea for the cost of the cheapest ticket. On 29 August, the paper, in a scathing attack, commented that it:

> '...looks like a determination to restrain the middle and humbler classes from enjoying the greatest musical treat... the rich have it all to themselves.'

Following a week of six separate concerts including the music of Beethoven, Mozart, Handel, Rossini, and Mendelssohn (of course) and others, the week concluded with a Grand Fancy Dress Ball.

Adverts from tailors and costumers - some of them from London - appeared in the press throughout the summer offering their services for a whole range of fancy dresses. The London apparel could be inspected at the Lyceum on Bold Street, the street which housed most of the fancy dress makers. On the evening, more than 300 individuals appeared appropriately attired. The *Mercury* on 4 September published a full list of names of those, and their attire, in attendance.

People appeared dressed as, for example, Swiss and French peasants, cavaliers, matadors, Hamlet, Don Juan, Walter Raleigh and Confucius. Kings were represented including Charles II, George III and Charles XII of Sweden, a monarch who was defeated in a disastrous war with Peter the Great of Russia. The *Mercury* declared the evening *'an unqualified success.'*

In 1933 a fire destroyed Cunningham's hall and it was replaced by the art deco style Philharmonic Hall of which twenty-first century audiences will be familiar.

* *

Fancy dress balls were very much part of the entertainment calendar of wealthy Liverpool citizens. On 25 March 1844, one such charitable event was held at the Town Hall. Three days earlier the *Mercury* outlined the rationale for the occasion.

> *'Liverpool is famed for its efforts in ameliorating the condition of its poorer inhabitants. It has been generous in supporting asylums wherein the sick, blind, homeless and starving could live in temporary care, succour and shelter. Institutions such as the Northern and Southern Hospitals have benefitted from charitable*

efforts, but the recent downturn has had an effect on their effectiveness. They and the Liverpool Infirmary, the Dispensaries (offering advice and assistance to the ailing) and the District Provident Society are now in great difficulty. A Grand Fancy Dress Ball will be held at the Town Hall to raise funds for such worthy institutions.'

The institutions relied on charitable donations for their existence, for example, some wealthy citizens made regular donations at weekly church services. On the evening of the ball, to aid the coffers of the beneficiaries, more than 1,000 people paid at least £1 each to attend. Like the report on the opening of the Philharmonic, the *Mercury* of 29 March gave a detailed account of all those attending. Beginning at 9.00 p.m. guests arrived depicting the usual kings, queens, peasants and many historical figures. *'The guests enjoyed refreshments including jellies, custards, tarts and pies; whilst port, sherry wine and lemonade were on offer'* the paper reported. The last guests departed at 4.00 a.m. and nearly £2,000 (about £180,000 in 2016) was raised at the event.

Charity

As indicated, some wealthy Victorian British citizens were renowned for their charity and philanthropy; one of the key characteristics of several philanthropists was the establishment of charitable foundations and institutions, several of which existed in Liverpool during the mid-nineteenth century.

Religion was integral to Victorian philanthropy. Religious establishments became increasingly involved in charitable endeavours with saving the poor being regarded as a Christian duty; a way of saving one's soul while helping those in need. To the deeply religious, everyone was deemed a child of God, so charitable works were a means to salvation for the *'needy'*. They may have been judged as being *'without God'*.

A key concept in Victorian attitudes towards poverty was that of the *'deserving'* and the *'undeserving'* poor. The deserving poor were those who were poor through no fault of their own, either because of illness, accident or age, or because there was no work available for them (perhaps because of a factory closure for example).

The undeserving poor were those who were in that position because they were portrayed as lazy or whose personal habits were problematical such as an inclination towards alcohol. Victorians were very concerned with how they could help the deserving poor without encouraging laziness in the undeserving poor. When Victorian charities were established their mission statements contained clear guidelines regarding who did and did not deserve to be assisted.

An examination of one prominent charitable institution, established in Liverpool in the 1840s, is evidential of the Victorian outlook on the deserving and undeserving nature of charity and the importance of religion to those in receipt of it. Early in 1840 a committee of Liverpool women issued a prospectus in which they appealed for public support for the foundation of a girls' orphan asylum. It was common knowledge that hundreds of young orphans were living on Liverpool streets., so, led by Anne Aikin, wife of Liverpool merchant and shipowner James Aikin (a portrait of whom hangs in the Walker Art Gallery), the women secured the financial support of a local accountant, Harmood Banner, and other wealthy Liverpool citizens.

A meeting of contributors and subscribers, chaired by the Mayor, Joshua Walmsley, took place in May 1840. Reported in the *Liverpool Mercury* on 12 May, the meeting resolved that the Liverpool Female Orphan Asylum would be *'of great value and utility'*. With religion a major component, the rules of admittance to the orphanage were strict:

> *'The children should be full orphans; they have to be of legitimate birth, live within seven miles of the Liverpool Exchange (Town Hall), be healthy, baptised in the Church of England and have no other means of support other than that provided by a workhouse.'*

Certificates had to be produced as proof of these conditions. *The Liverpool Stranger's Guide* (1844) added that the girls were to be:

> *'...removed from the risk of want and temptation... educated in a plain and suitable manner to fit them for domestic servants and apprenticed as household servants in the families of Guardians of the Institution or other respectable private families.'*

The plain and simple education was reading, writing, arithmetic and vocational skills. Daily religious services took place according to the principles of the Church of England.

A house was obtained at 97 Upper Stanhope Street; in August 1840 the first orphan, 10-year-old Mary Cearns, was admitted. Within a couple of years, with 40 girls in residence, the house was described as *'full to overflowing'*. In 1842 the Mayor, now Robertson Gladstone, laid the foundation stone of a new building in Myrtle Street offering more permanent accommodation for up to 150 girls, and on its opening in November 1843, 48 children were transferred from Upper Stanhope Street. In attendance at the opening were the Earl and

Countess of Sefton, the Mayor, Hugh McNeile, James Aikin, William Brown and Harmood Banner. An illustration of the orphanage was presented to Anne Aikin with inscription:

> 'To Mrs James Aikin, in testimony of her beneficence in projecting the Liverpool Female Orphan Asylum, and her zealous co-operation to render it successful, this view of the building is respectfully presented on the day of its opening, by the committee.'

The *Mercury* reported that:

> 'Mr James Aikin, in acknowledging on behalf of Mrs Aikin the compliment paid to her, was so overcome that he was unable to proceed. He said that when the heart was full it was difficult to give utterance to what was felt.'

Anne Aikin died in July 1849 aged 55, but the charitable work she started continued with the support of a substantial group of benefactors. In April 1850, a small boys' orphanage was established in a rented house at 21 Hope Street to which 22 children were admitted. However, to meet the need for larger premises equivalent to those provided for the orphan girls, the foundation stone for a boys' orphanage near to the girls' in Myrtle Street was laid by the Mayor, Thomas Littledale, in October 1852. This opened in March 1854. The orphanage's aims were the same as the girls with the boys often apprenticed to local firms by the age of 15.

Harmood Banner went on to purchase burial plots at nearby St. James Cemetery (which is situated close to the Anglican Cathedral) for several children who may have lost their lives whilst in residence at the orphanage. When the cemetery was eventually transformed into St James' Gardens, most of the headstones were removed;

however, there are still a number visible today. They reveal the names and ages of some very young children who passed away at both orphanages.

* *

Many well-established charities in Liverpool major concerns regarded women's welfare of women and in particular, prostitutes. One such charity, *The Benevolent Society for Reclaiming Unfortunate Ladies* (1838) based at 145 Mill Street, was anxious about *'the appalling monster evil of female prostitution.'* These words, delivered in a lecture entitled *Prostitution in the Borough of Liverpool* at the *Music Hall,* Bold Street on 3 June 1843 by the Reverend William Bevan of the *Newington Chapel,* were published in a pamphlet bearing the same title. Bevan told his audience that police Head Constable, Michael Whitty had provided him with data from 1842 which revealed 770 brothels or houses of *'bad character'* in Liverpool, which housed a total of 2,899 prostitutes known to the police.

Delivering his lecture on behalf of the Benevolent Society, Bevan, having first addressed what he argued were the causes and consequences of prostitution, outlined some of the aims of the institution, declaring:

> *'...the permanent reformation of females in prostitution cannot be hoped for, but on the grounds of their sound and scriptural conversion to God; the inmates shall attend regularly some place of worship and shall be met weekly by some pious or judicious persons to receive religious instruction.'*

He stated that since its commencement, 266 females had been received into the care of the society:

> '...of which 134 have been returned to their friends and have given permanent evidence of reformation, 17 respectfully married and 95 had voluntary left or had been dismissed.'

Bevan concluded by calling on Christians to work to save prostitutes:

> 'Jesus Christ came into the world to save sinners, why should this be withheld from the chief sinners, let them know that the door of refuge will never be closed.'

A similar institution, the *Magdalen Asylum*, otherwise known as the *Female Penitentiary* situated on Faulkner Street, was designed for the *'reception of penitent prostitutes.'* The *Stranger's Guide* stated that of the admissions in 1843 it was:

> 'Calculated that more than one third of all females received within walls have become good and reputable members of society.'

Married, pregnant, and close to giving birth, but struggling to find care, another group of women were deemed worthy of *'saving.'* Working specifically with these women were two Liverpool institutions, the well-established *Ladies Charity*, founded in 1792 and based in Parr St, and the *Institution for Married Lying-in Women* situated in Pembroke Place, founded in 1841. Gore's Liverpool Directory (1844) stated that the *Ladies Charity* was concerned with the; *'Relief of poor married women in childbirth in their own homes.'* The latter institution was designed to be:

> *'Open at all hours for the reception of married women about to be confined and whose circumstance are particularly needy.'*

A government report on *The Sanitary Conditions of the Towns of Lancashire* (1843) stated that the institution: *'...had only admitted 46 patients in its first full year.'*

The narrow rules of the institutions regarding the care and reception of *'married women,'* disregarded the welfare of young single women who received no support from either the state or charities. Unmarried women did though receive plenty of scorn and condemnation (see chapter on crime). Regularly condemned as immoral, many were often forced to give birth in streets, alleyways, cellars and brothels. Often through little fault of their own (a few of the women were single domestic servants who'd been made pregnant by a member of the household where they were employed) they found themselves thrown on to the street and alone to give birth, having been judged as unworthy of support.

One other religious institution focusing on the welfare of women was the Convent of the Sisters of Mercy established in Mount Vernon in 1843. *Gore's Directory* (1844) claimed the organisation was founded in Liverpool:

> *'...to administer to the corporal and spiritual wants of the poor. To the convent is attached a House of Mercy into which poor females of good character are admitted and trained up to the habits of virtue and industry, 300 of whom have been provided with suitable accommodation since the commencement... The convent is supported by charitable subscriptions and the profits of the laundry and needlework done by these poor servants.'*

**

Established in 1829, *The Society for Promoting the Religious Improvement of the Poor of Liverpool and the Neighbourhood* by some 40 wealthy Christian businessmen and ministers in *'response to the poverty and squalid living conditions'* went on to, arguably, become Liverpool's largest charitable organisation. Based originally in Slater Street and later in Lord Street its rather cumbersome title was later shortened to *The Liverpool Christian Instruction Society* and in 1837 it became the *Liverpool Town Mission*. Eventually when Liverpool was given its city status it changed its name to the *Liverpool City Mission*.

Two directors of the *Liverpool to Manchester Railway Company*, James Cropper and Adam Hodgson, were among the institution's founding members. Both men were well known for their Protestant religious zeal. For example, the City Mission's official history (*A Voice in the City: 150 Years History* of the *Liverpool City Mission*: Gordon Read and David Jebson: 1980) states that Cropper *'believed the bible from cover to cover.'* Other committee members included banker Samuel Hope (the famous street takes its name from his family), John Gladstone, father of the future Prime Minister William, and from 1844-48 Dr William Henry Duncan. The mission's object was:

> *'to promote the Religious improvement of the poor and needy, especially of such as do not attend the public services of Divine Worship.'*

The mission was closely associated with another charitable organisation, the *District Provident Society* housed in Queen Square. The society's first report (1830) stated its aim included *'...the encouragement of industry and frugality and the suppression of mendacity.'*

The organisation sent out workers to visit the poor to encourage them to make small deposits to be redeemed later and spent on necessities such as clothes, fuel, rent, plus *'the purchase of bibles.'* The society did though dispense food relief in special circumstances. For example, in the years 1842 and 1843 19,462 people applied for relief, of whom 500 were refused as being undeserving of support.

A group of Protestants, the Unitarians, were very active in the *Town Mission*. Unitarianism was viewed as having an open-minded and individualistic approach to religion, giving scope to a wide range of beliefs and doubts. Amongst the Unitarians was William Rathbone. Unitarians believed religion should be broad, inclusive, and tolerant. Unitarianism could therefore include people who were not just Christian but of other religious beliefs such as Judaism for example. In 1836, on behalf of the mission, Rathbone addressed a congregation of Unitarians at the Unitarian Chapel on Renshaw Street. Margaret Simey in her 1992 book *Charity Rediscovered* reports his words, he said; *'There is in existence in Liverpool no fewer than 60,000 individuals who pass from childhood to age without any efficient means of religious culture.'* He added, the mission should:

> *'exert itself to improve the moral and social conditions of these individuals and promote the religious improvement and moral and social conditions of the poor.'*

The Mission employed what it called *'missioners'* to work the streets of Liverpool. Rathbone pledged that its missioners would become *'Christian advisers to the poor.'* These were paid up to £40 per year remunerated from the subscriptions of its members. The missioners originally visited the courts and cellars of Liverpool poorest districts around Tithebarn Street, Leeds Street and Great Crosshall Street. By the 1840s, 21 were engaged in the roles and according to the modern *City Mission* website the:

'Agents' would visit homes all over the city on behalf of the mission to read the bible and explain the way of salvation to those who were unable to find a home in the established churches of the day... The purpose of the Mission was to bring practical help and support to poor families and to preach the good news of Jesus Christ.'

Given specific streets to visit the missioners were under strict instructions of what they should and should not do. Read and Jebson say that they were:

'...to be wise, tactful and patient. They were not to attack the Roman Catholic Church and engage in dispute, but to spread the message of the Bible. They were however to testify against all open sin such as drunkenness, uncleanliness, cruelty in parents and disobedience in children. They were to encourage people to read the Bible in their families and to attend church.'

The missioners were to keep journals of all their visits and to present them to the mission committee monthly. From these journals, published in the book above, evidence emerges of the difficulties faced by the missioners and more so by the families they visited. In 1842 one missioner, who brought food with him, reported on a morning's visit to the south of the town. A sample of his report includes:

> *'Mann Street – blacksmith, four weeks out of work, family of four, pledged (pawned) nearly all their clothes and furniture to buy food'*

> *'Fisher Street – labourer, ten weeks without work, wife and two children who have been two days without food, their last meal being a loaf of bread. They have pledged everything and have neither clothes nor bedclothes'*

The missioner's report goes on to cover a total of twenty families he visited on that morning alone; virtually all suffering similar problems. He distributed *'bread, meal and potatoes in different quantities to each family he visited.'* Interestingly he makes no mention of spreading the word of the Bible.

The principal agent or missioner in the 1840s was another Unitarian, the Reverend John Johns. Margaret Simey says that Johns, born in Plymouth in 1801, began his work with zest, travelling the poorest districts, entering homes, reading from the bible, attempting to spread moral and spiritual guidance in the hope of those receiving would achieve religious self-improvement.

In his 1841 report, Johns described the cellars in which many lived as *'graves inhabited by the living.'* Over time the experience of life in some parts of Liverpool started to have a profound effect on him and, says Simey, spreading the message of the Bible decreased. By 1847, she adds, as more and more victims of the Irish potato famine arrived in Liverpool, he now believed the spiritual component of his work was futile. Reproducing details from one of his reports, Simey writes of the *'horrors'* Johns witnessed.

> *'More and more families crammed into already overcrowded cellars and courts. Houses of the lowest classes were so crowded*

during this period that it was common to find every apartment of a dwelling occupied by several families. The father, the mother and the children sleeping together in one corner; the father, the mother the children of another family sleeping together in another corner. And so on and so on.'

Johns became a member of the District Provident Society in 1845 and was now involved in issuing food tickets on its behalf. He wrote *'Day after day and week after week crowds of applicants besieged the door of your office lobby, stairs and landings and out into the street.'* Simey states that Johns came to believe that it was *'bread alone which the poor required not moral guidance.'*

On 23 June 1847, after visiting more areas of the town, John Johns, a married father of two children, died having succumbed to the typhus fever epidemic which was decimating parts of Liverpool that year. Margaret Simey concludes that Johns considered that *'people's physical improvement was primary and only when this was achieved could spiritual improvement be achieved.'* John Johns was the only non-Catholic churchman to die of typhus that summer. Thousands attended his funeral. The Unitarian Church in Ullett Road bears a plaque in memorial to his life and work on behalf of the mission.

4. Crime and Punishment

Liverpool was no different to any other British metropolitan town when it came to crime and disorder, however the government and the Home Office in particular was increasingly turning its attention to the challenges faced by criminals and criminal offences. Beginning in Britain in 1829 the maintenance of law and order was changing as towns and cities established their own local police forces, but in Liverpool this was no easy matter.

The Head Constable struggled to build a competent, reliable police service as many of his newly employed officers showed a preference for drink rather than doing their duty. Regarding the administration of justice, both the magistrate and assize courts were busy dealing with offences ranging from relatively minors acts of theft, for example, to murder cases of which one in 1849 in particular was so horrific it captured the attention and imagination of the country. Questions though can be asked regarding how justice was administered in such cases.

There were two prisons in Liverpool during the 1840s and neither solely used to deny people freedom. physical punishment was administered daily and many prisoners were sentenced to hard labour. The prisons were also holding houses for those awaiting transportation to Australia. The ultimate punishment, the death penalty, was handed down to those convicted of murder and in Liverpool, this was carried out in public outside the Kirkdale House of Correction.

Individuals belonging to one particular group of people sometimes faced the possibility of the death penalty. Young, single women, who had lost their children soon after giving birth often found themselves charged with murder. When pregnant, many of these young women were often turned out of their homes by their families or on occasion, if employed as domestic servants, by their employers. Alone and desperate, the women were forced to give birth in any place that allowed. Predictably many children tragically died and if discovered the women could be charged with infanticide, the murder of a child. There were dozens of such cases coming before the courts in 1840s Liverpool.

Policing

In 1829, Home Secretary, Robert Peel established the Metropolitan Police Force in London. The new force superseded the local 'Watch' in the London area. The watch did not cover all areas of the capital, so Peel's intention was for the new force to do just that.
The Liverpool Town Council established its Police Force along similar lines to the Metropolitan in 1836, replacing two forces, the Night Watch and the Corporation Constabulary (day police). In 1841, the independent Dock Watch amalgamated with the Liverpool Police.

Liverpool was separated into two divisions, with stations in the north of the town at Rose Hill, and in the south, on Seel Street. Both divisions contained bridewells at Exchange Street East and Vauxhall Road in the north and in the south at Brick Street and Duncan Street East.
Pay and conditions for constables, even by mid-nineteenth century standards, were not fantastic. Officers earned 18 shillings per week for six twelve-hour days.

The new police force though inherited many problems associated with the previous forces. According to Joe Hellier at liverpoolcitypolice.com:

> 'None of the aforementioned organisations had particularly good reputations. The Night Watch in particular had a reputation for being drunkards... In 1835 the Watch Committee reported that the behaviour of the police had 'progressively improved' as there had only been 639 cases of drunkenness and 1,592 other disciplinary offences recorded that year against police officers out of a force of 574!'

The establishment of new police force failed to immediately eradicate these problems. In 1838 it reported the dismissal of 25 officers for being drunk on duty; 19 for being the worse for liquor and being in public houses when on duty; three for being asleep on their beats; 15 for being absent from their beats and neglect of duty; three for being the worse for drink when off duty. A further 160 officers were fined or reduced in rank for being drunk on duty.

If they were to create an effective, responsible police service, commanders needed to overcome these serious cultural problems. A slow process, but the situation did gradually improve in the 1840s, as new recruits were more aware of their responsibilities and duties, but, Hellier says, it was not really until the end of the nineteenth century that a fully effective force was in operation.

The Liverpool Police Force's first three Head constables were Michael Whitty (1836-44), Henry Miller (1844-45) and Mathew Dowling (1845-52). Irish born Whitty arrived in Liverpool in 1829 to work as a journalist on the *Liverpool Journal*, where he wrote many articles on crime in the town. In 1833 he was appointed, Superintendent of the

Night Watch. When the Liverpool Police Force was established three years later, he was promoted to Head Constable. Whitty was responsible for recruiting and organising the new police force and he placed adverts in the local press calling for new constables. Most of the 360 recruits were, however, drawn from the pre-established forces.

Replacing Whitty, Henry Miller's period as Head Constable was short-lived, he resigned after serving less than a year in post. Mathew Dowling, his replacement, arguably became the force's most famous Head Constable. A Londoner, Dowling was heading the Lambeth Division of the Metropolitan Police, when in 1833 he was offered the post of Superintendent of the Liverpool Dock Police. In post, he trained and qualified as a barrister before succeeding Miller as head of the Liverpool Police. barrister was appointed Head Constable upon Miller's departure from the post.

Courts

In the 1840s there were three types of court; the magistrates, petty sessions and, for more serious offences such as murder, the assize courts (the equivalent of today's crown court). Serious cases would first be heard at the magistrate's, which would then refer them to the assizes.

At the coroner's court, judgements were made on the cause and manner of all suspicious deaths. If the court deemed the deceased a victim of murder, if able to, the coroner had powers to question the accused. If he believed there was a case to answer, he would then send him or her to the assizes.

The magistrate's court presided over the great majority of relatively less serious court cases such as theft, robbery and assault. The magistrate controlled the court, questioning defendants and witnesses before announcing a verdict. In 1840s Liverpool, the chief, stipendiary magistrate was Edward Rushton. Born in 1795, his more famous father, also named Edward, was a poet, anti-slave trade campaigner and co-founder of the country's first School for the Blind, which opened in London Road in 1791.

Prior to qualifying as a barrister and being called to the bar in 1831, Rushton junior began his working life as a printer and stationer. He was appointed Stipendiary Magistrate of Liverpool by the town council in May 1839. His appointment, not fully supported, divided councillors with Liberal politicians in favour and many Tories in opposition. Rushton was a proponent of prison reform, including the humane treatment of juvenile offenders. Alternatively, he was opposed to capital punishment. Forthright in his opinions, Rushton often clashed with other local institutions such as the press and Liverpool Workhouse.

Coming under the scope of capital crime, assize courts judges dealt with serious offences such as murder, conspiracy, rape, forgery and treason, those that and verdicts were returned by locally picked juries of 12 men (no women). In major towns or counties and known as quarterly sessions, assize courts were held four times a year, one for each season. Depending on the number of cases, sessions could run over several days. If there was pressure to conduct business sometimes a special quarter was added to the calendar.

Assize Court procedure began with the prosecution presenting the case against the defendant. Witnesses would then be called. The prosecution case was usually heavily dependent on witnesses with the judge often intervening to ask questions or make comments. Defendants would often defend themselves, calling their own witnesses to try to prove their innocence. In offences such as murder, the defendant was granted a defence barrister or attorney to act on their behalf. In many murder trials defendants rarely gave evidence, their barrister often advised against doing so, as will be seen in some Liverpool examples.

Although on the rare occasion a murder court case could last a couple of days, most trials were over in a few minutes. With the evidence concluded the judge would then sum up. A defendant's criminal history could also be read out and heard by the jury who would then be asked to consider its verdict. More often than not, this would take place without the jury leaving its box.

Often before the case went to court, the Liverpool press covered many murder cases in great detail, devoting thousands of words for their readers to dissect, for example examining the backgrounds of the alleged offender and offering opinions on their character.

Prisons

In the 1840s Liverpool contained two prisons. The oldest, the *Borough Gaol* on Great Howard Street near to the north docks, opened in 1786. The street is named after the prison reformer, John Howard, who, in 1777, condemned the British prison system for being disorganised, barbaric and filthy. He called for wide-ranging reforms including paid staff, outside inspections, a proper diet and other necessities. The government introduced some of his recommendations by the 1780s.

Prisons underwent regular government inspections and one such took place in the Borough Jail in October 1845. The previous year a total of 16,214 people had served their sentences in the Great Howard Street jail, 1,337 of them for drunkenness. At the time of the inspection there were 505 prisoners interned with 277 sentenced to additional hard labour. 84 of the 195 female prisoners, were convicted of prostitution and were handed sentences ranging from seven days to one month, except for three women awaiting transportation to Australia. A *'serial offender,'* the oldest of the three women was 57. The inspector visited the women's reception ward where he found *'three together in a cell in a very disorderly condition.'* The prison chaplain informed him that sometimes up to five women would occupy these cells which were designed for just one inmate.

The inspector interviewed teenage prisoners on the male wing. One boy, identified as JT and aged 15, was in prison for the fifth time. He said his father had died and his mother had since married a baker, gone leaving him to fend for himself. He consequently spent time in the workhouse. He told the inspector that he wanted to leave Britain, so he *'tried stowing away on a New York bound ship'*, but was soon discovered and returned to Liverpool. His wish was *'to go to the West Indies'*, but the boy feared he would most likely end up in the workhouse once more. He said the prison regime was very strict and inmates could have their food stopped for *'laughing at the supper table or in the prison yard, talking in the workrooms or singing in their cells.'*

Owing to the rapid rise in the town's population, one prison was deemed inadequate to hold the numbers now being sentenced to jail. In 1817 the government commissioned the building of the *Kirkdale*

House of Correction which opened in 1821. As the name indicates, punishment was to be the key element of imprisonment there. Simple loss of liberty, imprisonment, was the sentence handed down to most prisoners. However, despite Howard's concerns, hard labour and physical punishment were often recommended by judges. Hard labour included:

Oakum picking: this form of labour involved convicts pulling apart old ships' ropes by hand. When suitable, the ropes were then sold on. It was boring, unpleasant work that made fingers bleed and blister. The oakum picked by convicts is said to be the origin of the phrase *'money for old rope.'*

The treadmill: this relatively new form of hard labour was introduced in 1817 with one of its kind constructed inside Kirkdale. A large wheel on which prisoners walked, the treadmill was designed to control a millstone turning wheat into flour. The punishment was abolished in British prisons in 1898.

Shot drill: this involved prisoners carrying cannon balls across a prison yard or passing them along the line to each other. This too was often used at Kirkdale.

Whipping: Finally, a judge could sentence a convict to be whipped. No rules appear to have been laid down as to how it was carried out. In practice, it generally seems to have been administered to the upper back. On 7 April 1843, the *Liverpool Mercury* reported the words of Kirkdale's chaplain, the Reverend Richard Appleton, who said *'I believe a sound whipping for juvenile offenders is good for helping them to reform.'* The whipping of females was abolished in 1820.

Some sentences went beyond hard labour and physical punishment including transportation and the ultimate penalty, execution.

Transportation: Up until 1830 transportation was viewed as an alternative to hanging. The death penalty could be handed down for dozens of offences including theft. After that date many offences were removed from the death penalty, but remained for transportation. In the 18th century convicts were transported to America to serve their sentences. Following the American War of Independence, this ended in 1787.

Australia, and to a lesser extent Bermuda, became the future destination for convicted criminals. From the viewpoint of the authorities, transportation was practical and efficient as it was advantageous in removing criminals from British society and in being relatively cheap. Additionally, the chances of a convict returning to Britain were quite slim. The minimum sentence was seven years, but many convicts received 14 year sentences. Having served their sentences, therefore, many convicts remained in Australia.

The use of transportation began to reduce dramatically in the 1850s and it was eventually abolished in 1868. The 1840s was, therefore, the last major decade for transportation. At Liverpool assizes, during one day in the summer of 1842, 39 people were sentenced to transportation, all of them for theft. Their ages ranged from 12 to 48. The majority were teenagers and they were evenly split in terms of males and females. The minimum sentence administered was seven years and the maximum life. Examples of convicts transported:

Timothy Callaghan - 18 - stealing a pair of boots – life (his third offence)

Samuel Huxley – 48 – stealing a waistcoat, knife and comb - 14 years

Mary Ann Jones – Stealing a set of beads and a pinafore – 10 years

Elizabeth Roberts and Price Parker – both 18 – stealing 'money' 7 years.

Counterfeiting was another crime for which transportation issued. In April 1843 seven men aged from 17 to 43 years of age were all given sentences of seven years' transportation for making or possessing counterfeit coins.

Death penalty: In 1840s Britain hundreds of people were sentenced to death and their executions were carried out in public often in front of huge crowds enjoying a festive atmosphere. Public executions were more akin to fun fairs, with sideshows and food and drink available. Newspapers would carry detailed accounts of trials and executions. There was a growing trade too in the execution 'broadsides', usually single sheets containing details of the crime and the condemned's 'last confession' and final words.

The authorities believed that public executions acted as a deterrent to murder by terrifying onlookers. Crowds, by the mid-nineteenth century at least, didn't appear to be terrified by a public execution, in fact there is plenty of evidence to suggest that they appeared to look forward to a *good hanging.* The occasions also offered perfect opportunities for pickpockets and other criminals to ply their trades.

The behaviour of many at these events disgusted many observers, including Charles Dickens for example, who called for the abolition of public executions. In the 1840s Dickens attended several hangings, including one in 1849 of Mr and Mrs Manning which took place at Southwark in London. The Mannings had murdered a friend for his money and buried him under their kitchen floor. The newspapers billed it as *'the hanging of the century'* being the first of a husband and wife together. Dickens joined a crowd of 30,000, renting a room in a house close to the prison. Having viewed the spectacle. on 13 November, he wrote to the *Times*:

> 'I believe that a sight so inconceivably awful as the wickedness and levity of the immense crowd collected at that execution this morning could be imagined by no man... When the day dawned, thieves, low prostitutes, ruffians, and vagabonds of every kind, flocked on to the ground, with every variety of offensive and foul behaviour. Fightings, faintings, whistlings, brutal jokes, tumultuous demonstrations of indecent delight when swooning women were dragged out of the crowd by the police, with their dresses disordered, gave a new zest to the general entertainment.'

The death penalty itself was a great source of debate and its use and efficacy was contested in the local and national press. The *Liverpool Mercury,* opposed to its use, vied on regular occasions with a proponent, the *Liverpool Albion*. The London *Times* though was positively in favour of its use. One editorial of June 1847 entitled The Economy of the Scaffold declared:

> 'A length of stout cord costs less than two years in prison or seven years' transportation. Hanging is in fact cheaper. The death of a convict saves at once his supervision and his keep.'

Other groups such as the Peace Society a largely religious organisation formed earlier in the century, campaigned not only against war, but also against the death penalty. A Liverpool branch of the society, including members such as councillor and health campaigner, William Rathbone and Stipendiary Magistrate, Edward

Rushton, was established in the town in the 1830s. In August 1844, the branch organised a petition to be submitted to parliament calling for the abolition of the death penalty. It was presented to the government by the notable nineteenth century MP and society member, John Bright. The petition argued that the:

> '...death penalty is ineffective as a protection to the public, is productive to the increase in crime and is contrary to the spirit of Christianity on which our laws are founded.'

It further added that public executions were *'revolting, brutalising and demoralising.'*

Prior to the nineteenth century, many public hangings in Liverpool were carried out in the area of what is now London Road, but as the century turned and the town grew, they were transferred to the fields outside Kirkdale Prison, having enough space to accommodate over 100,000 people.

In its opposition, the *Mercury* took every opportunity to vehemently express its condemnation of the practice. On 6 May 1843 two people, Wilmot Buckley of St Helens, for the murder of his wife, and Betty Eccles of Manchester, for poisoning her stepson, were hanged in public at Kirkdale. The paper, estimating a crowd of around 40,000 in attendance, wrote:

> *'From an early hour in the morning the approaches to the gaol were crowded by dense masses of individuals, chiefly of the most dissolute orders who indulged in coarse jests, cursing, swearing, laughing and joking. The scene was one of the most disgusting description. Carts and coaches loaded with the inmates of brothels*

drove up to the spot and Scotland Road bore much of the same appearance as it does on raceday.'

The petitions of the Peace Society, Charles Dickens' protestations and the Mercury pleas didn't effect parliament. It would take a couple of decades for an amendment to the law, when in 1868 public executions were banned.

Poachers on Lord Derby's Knowsley Estate

On the evening of 9 November 1843, 19-year-old Naaman Shaw of Eldon Street and John Roberts, 26, of Limekiln Lane met in the Cattle Market public house on London Road. Both Vauxhall men were regular poachers, Shaw having being taught the art by his father John. Along with several friends, the men planned to go poaching that evening on Lord Derby's Knowsley estate.

Lord Derby, Edward Smith-Stanley, had been MP for Preston and Lancashire from 1796 to 1832. In 1834 he succeeded his father as 13th Earl of Derby and withdrew from politics to instead concentrate on his natural history collection at Knowsley Hall. In the grounds of his estate he kept a large assortment of live animals and game birds such as pheasants and quails on which Shaw, Roberts and their associates had set their sights. To deal with the threat of poaching, Derby, employed a six-man team of gamekeepers to protect his stock.

After a few beers, Shaw and Roberts made their way from London Road up to Old Swan and then Knotty Ash to pick up their accomplices, James Hunt, Henry Fillingham, Thomas Jacques, Joseph Rimmer and four others men. The poachers carried three guns and several sticks between them. Naaman Shaw was to say later that he met his father, John, in Knotty Ash who warned him of the presence of gamekeepers on the estate and advised him against poaching that evening.

In the early hours of the 10 November, the poachers entered Lord Derby's grounds in what is now part of the Huyton estate. By around 4.30 a.m. they had bagged three pheasant, but gunshots had alerted the gamekeepers to their activity who tracked their whereabouts and lay in wait in a ditch. Coming into view, the poachers were confronted. Four shots rang out; two from the poachers and two from the gamekeepers. One of the gamekeepers, Richard Kenyon, a married father of two children, was hit in the stomach.

The poachers fled and the badly wounded Kenyon was carried off. He died four days later from his wounds. Head gamekeeper, James Tyrer, believed he identified one of the poachers as John Shaw, father of Naaman. John Shaw, who in the non-too distant past worked as a gamekeeper on the Derby estate, was very familiar to Tyrer. The police, with the Tyrer's information, arrested John Shaw and charged him with murder. A short while later he was committed for trial.

Speaking at his committal trial before stipendiary magistrate Edward Rushton, Shaw informed the court that he could provide witnesses to prove he was elsewhere on the night and following morning of the murder. His son, Naaman, was one of those who could confirm the alibi.
Following an interview with Shaw junior, the police chose to drop the prosecution of his father. Instead they offered a reward of £100 (real price value of about £9,000 in 2016), plus the promise of a Queen's pardon, for anyone offering information leading to the prosecution of any person connected to the crime. Naaman Shaw came forward to

help the police with their enquiries and several arrests subsequently followed.

On 26 December 1843, the trial of those apprehended began in Liverpool. John Roberts was charged with murder and Fillingham, Hunt, Jacques and Rimmer were charged with aiding and abetting; all pleaded not guilty. The other four gang members were not apprehended. Naaman Shaw, when called to provide evidence, was in court as an *'approver'*, a term used in old English law which referred to: *'an accomplice to a crime who confesses their guilt and gives evidence against their collaborators'*.

James Tyrer and two other gamekeepers were first to give evidence. Tyrer described how he heard the gunshots and gathered his team to confront the poachers. As they did, Tyrer said he recognised the voice of John Shaw. He cried out *"Jack Shaw is that thee*?" As he did, however, he heard a cry of *"shoot 'em"* from the poachers and a shot rang out. Tyrer ordered one of his gamekeepers to return fire, which he did.

Fearing for their lives, both the poachers and gamekeepers fled the scene. Moments later, Tyrer realised that Kenyon had been shot and wounded. The gamekeepers carried Kenyon to his lodgings to receive medical attention, but he never recovered and died four days later. Called next to give evidence were the other gamekeepers and they corroborated that of their boss.

Appearing as an approver, Naaman Shaw was next on the stand. He told the court how the group, ten of them in total, gathered on the evening before the murder, but without his father who advised the gang not to carry out their plan. When he confronted the gang, Tyrer, must have mistaken another gang member for his father, said

Naaman Shaw. Shaw then told the court that he, Roberts and Fillingham carried the guns and when confronted one of their group cried "*shoot 'em.*" It was Roberts, he said, who fired the two shots, one of which hit Kenyon.

On the advice of their barrister, Mr Taylor, none of the defendants were called to give evidence in their own defence, Taylor preferring to attempt to persuade the jury that Naaman Shaw was an untrustworthy individual, who was out to protect his, and his father's skins. Without Naaman Shaw's testimony, Taylor contended, the prosecution's case falls apart. Moreover, it was the Shaws in fact who were the murderers and not his clients. Being very familiar with him, Tyrer was not mistaken in his recognition of John Shaw, Taylor concluded.

Before making his closing statement, the judge asked the defendants if any of them wanted to address the court. Hunt merely said that he was innocent and Rimmer said he had an alibi to prove he was a gang member. The other three declined to speak.

The judge began his summation, but part way through he was informed that two witnesses, husband and wife George and Mary Jacques (brother and sister-in-law of defendant Thomas Jacques), had come forward to provide an alibi for Rimmer. Mary told the court that Rimmer was a lodger and that on the night before the murder she went to bed at 11.00 pm leaving the defendant and her husband sitting and talking. Bizarrely though, George Jacques contradicted his wife, saying he had gone to bed at 9.30, which left Rimmer's alibi in tatters. Prosecuting barrister, Brandt, declared that the Jacques' testimony was, 'An unsuccessful attempt at an alibi that strengthened the case against Rimmer.'

The judge returned to and completed his summing up and the jury retired to consider its verdicts. Within a few minutes, it returned guilty verdicts on all five and the judge condemned the men to death. Their executions by hanging were scheduled to take place at Kirkdale on 20 January 1844. The judge did though say he would pass on their pleas for mercy to the Home Secretary, Sir James Graham.

The convicted men received lots of support in Liverpool, not least from the local press. Although it fully accepted the men guilty of killing Kenyon, the *Mercury* was vehemently opposed to a murder conviction. The paper felt at best the charge should have been one of manslaughter, arguing that the poachers did not enter Lord Derby's estate with murder in mind. It wrote *'Roberts fired the shot in the belief that he was going to be shot.'* The *Mercury,* along with another Liverpool newspaper the *Journal*, called for a commutation of the sentences to transportation for life.

The *Mercury* organised a petition claiming the *'Liverpool populace is fully behind our position.'* Despite petitioning the government, the paper nevertheless did not have great faith in overturning the verdict. Home Secretary, James Graham, was regarded as a stern, stubborn man. The satirical magazine *Punch*, for example, claimed that:

> *'Home Secretaries were hard-hearted, more especially Sir James Graham, a most pitiless man, possessed by a great belief in hanging.'*

Graham was a fervent advocate of capital punishment as a deterrent. The previous year for instance, much to the disbelief of many, he ignored pleas for mercy in the case of an 84-year-old Scotsman, Allan Mair, convicted of murdering his 85-year-old wife. Mair said he wanted to end his wife's suffering. Graham approved the execution of the oldest man in British history. Hopes for the five men were, therefore, not high.

However, whilst in prison waiting on Graham's decision, Roberts admitted to firing the fatal shot. Reported in the press, he blamed alcohol, saying he spent most of the day drinking, was intoxicated at the time and incapable of making a rational decision. After his conviction, he turned to God, prayed daily and attended the prison chapel. Roberts confessed to murder to the prison chaplain saying he deeply regretted his actions and expressed sympathy to the Kenyon family. He said he was *'truly repentant.'* On the 12 January, just eight days before execution, there was good news for four of the defendants. Home Secretary, Graham had commuted the sentences of Fillingham, Hunt, Jacques and Rimmer to transportation for life. Roberts though was not as fortunate; his execution was to go ahead as planned.

At 12.00 noon on Saturday 20 January, in front of a reported 30,000 people, Roberts was brought to the scaffold. Allowed to address the crowd, he said:

> 'I have prayed very hard for forgiveness. I hope good people that you will turn from your sins and wickedness. The Lord bless you all. The Lord have mercy upon my soul.'

Moments later Roberts was hanged and as the executioner was cutting down his body, the *Mercury* reported that: *'…some of the crowd behaved in a riotous and unbecoming manner.'* Several large stones were thrown at the executioner. The paper added that the crowd's behaviour: *'…had been much worse than that at recent public hangings at Kirkdale.'* At Roberts' execution, unlike at most public hangings, the target of the crowd's anger was not the murderer but the executioner.

The *Liverpool Journal,* though in condemnation of the crowd's behaviour, empathised with its feelings. Believing the crowd attacked the executioner and not the condemned man because many within it sympathised with poachers, the claimed that *'primitive game laws added to the multiplication of crime and criminals.'* It added that the aristocracy bred and fattened pheasant for game hunters, claiming:

> *'Half a county is depopulated in order that a privileged aristocracy might be amused... pheasants have replaced the peasants and the county gaols are filled with poachers.'*

Poachers, it seems, had much support. The *Journal* believed that Roberts had little chance of a reprieve saying Graham had to be seen to be delivering the severest punishment to at least one person associated with the crime. The answer will never be known, but did Roberts finally confess to murder in an attempt to save the lives of his fellow poachers?

The Leveson Street Outrage

At approximately 11.00 a.m. on the morning of March 26 1849, eight months pregnant Anne Hinrichson, the wife of a sea captain, left her home on Leveson St in the south of the town, to undertake a shopping trip. Returning home, and entering her hallway, she was attacked and beaten with a blunt instrument, probably a poker. Also attacked shortly before her arrival home, were Mrs Hinrichson's two children, aged five and three, and her maid, Mary Parr aged 29. The victims were quickly discovered by family associates who reported the tragedy to the police.

Forensic officers entered the bloodied scene and were able to determine that blunt instruments had been used on the eldest child and Mary Parr, while the youngest child, who was dead at the scene, was a victim of a knife attack. They also discovered a jewellery box which they believed had been forced open and some items, including a watch had been stolen.

Within 24 hours Anne Hinrichson and her eldest child had died because of their dreadful injuries. Though very badly injured, Mary Parr was still alive and under treatment at the Southern Hospital and was able to furnish the police with a great deal of information relating to the family and the horrific events.

In 1848, John Hinrichson of Hull was appointed captain of a Liverpool based ship, the SS Duncan, so the family left their east coast home to move to Leveson Street, Toxteth. At the end of 1848 John was commanding his ship on a long sea journey, leaving his wife to look after the family home. To try to increase income, Anne, an accomplished pianist, began to teach lessons. For further revenue, she also decided to take in lodgers and placed an advert in her front window.

On the eve of the murders, 26-year-old John Gleeson Wilson, having seen the advert, called at Leveson Street. Meeting Mrs Hinrichson, Gleeson Wilson told her that he was working in the dock yards as a ship's carpenter. Accepting his word, and one week's rent in advance, she let him a bedroom and the back parlour. Supplied with this news, the police had their prime suspect.

It quickly emerged that John Gleeson Wilson was actually Maurice Gleeson an Irishman from county Limerick. He left there, like many of his fellow countrymen and women during the terrible potato famine year of 1847. He first moved to Plymouth, which was followed by a short stay in London before he moved to Liverpool in 1848.
He first rented lodgings in Sparling St, close to the Albert Dock, where he married his landlady in December of that year. He was a violent man and his wife left him and went to live with her father in Tranmere, Wirral. The police could find no evidence of Gleeson Wilson having been employed in Liverpool., though they did learn that he was already in lodgings in Porter Street, Vauxhall, about a mile and a half from Leveson Street.

Mary Parr was able to give an account of the terrible events on the morning of the murder. She said Mrs Hinrichson went shopping between 10.00 and 11.00 am and Gleeson Wilson was at home. In a long statement, re-written by the police for the press, Mary Parr reported:

> *'The children were in the parlour and he drove them out with a newspaper, she was cleaning the grate when he came in to the parlour and asked her the price of fire tongs, the price of a fender and card tables. He then struck her on the head with the fire tongs. She said she did not remember anything else other than the children being in the room and lying there.'*

Mary Parr's evidence incriminated Gleeson Wilson and the police immediately set about tracking him down. They were successful; two days later he was apprehended.

Gleeson Wilson was brought to the southern Hospital where Marry Parr was asked to identify as the lodger and assailant. In the company of several police officers, the mayor, Thomas Bramley Moore and chief magistrate, Edward Rushton, Mary pointed to Gleeson Wilson and stated, *"That is the man with the hat on."* News had spread of Gleeson Wilson's appearance at the hospital and, upon leaving, he had to be protected from a baying mob. Mary Parr's condition worsened and she finally succumbed to her dreadful injuries, dying on 5 April.

In the meantime, Gleeson Wilson found himself at an identity parade, before appearing at the Magistrate's Court on Saturday 31 March. Several witnesses were brought forward to provide evidence of the defendant's movements on the day of the murder. First to do so were shop boys, Anthony Carney and Edward McDermott, who had said they both saw Gleeson Wilson on the morning of the murder; Michael Caine who saw Gleeson Wilson in nearby Toxteth Park; three cab drivers situated at the end of Leveson St.; a pawnbroker's assistant from London Road, who said that Gleeson Wilson attempted to sell him a watch; Mr Finn, also a pawnbroker of Great Homer Street and a shopkeeper in Great Howard Street.

The court heard that three of the witnesses had picked out Gleeson Wilson at an identity parade. Compelling enough, the magistrate committed Gleeson Wilson to trial at the next assizes.

Before the murder trial, however, a coroner's inquest took place on 2 April in front of Borough Coroner, Philip Finch Curry. The witnesses at the magistrate's court, plus a couple more who came forward later, gave evidence to the coroner. After hearing the evidence against him, Gleeson Wilson was allowed to question the witnesses and offer up a defence. He said the witnesses who claimed they saw him were mistaken and offered an alibi.

He told the coroner that he spent most of the morning and afternoon of the murder with Thomas Collopy, his landlord of Porter Street. Collopy was brought before the coroner but refuted Gleeson Wilson's alibi saying they were together the day after the murder. Gleeson Wilson did not deny trying to sell the watch, but said that it belonged to him. Having heard from witnesses and Gleeson Wilson, the 16-man coroner's jury concluded that the Hinrichson family had been the victims of murder and that the perpetrator was Gleeson Wilson.

Gleeson Wilson's trial began on 31 August with barrister, Sergeant Wilkins, opening the case for the prosecution. Explaining Mrs Hinrichson's final hours, Wilkins said that around 10 a.m. on the morning of the murder she had gone shopping in nearby Great George Street and James Street. There she purchased goods at different shops but, due to her advanced state of pregnancy, asked if they could be delivered to her home.

First witness, delivery boy Anthony Carney, told the court that around 11.00 he called at 20 Leveson Street to deliver a basket of potatoes. He said Gleeson Wilson opened the door, took the basket from him and returned it to him a few seconds later. He left and passed Mrs Hinrichson a few yards from her front door. Carney had picked out Gleeson Wilson at the identity parade.

Another delivery boy, Daniel Roebuck, was next up and he said that at around 11.15 he attempted to deliver two jugs which Anne Hinrichson earlier purchased. Roebuck told the court that he could not obtain an answer, but said he heard moaning coming from inside. Concerned, he peered through the door and saw a lady lying on the floor and assumed Mrs Hinrichson had fainted. He went to fetch a policeman. He returned with a constable, but by this time neighbours, responding to the noise from one of Mrs Hinrichson's piano pupils knocking on the door, had already broken in and discovered the bloody scene.

Three surgeons next explained the nature and state of the horrific injuries. Each victim suffered head wounds, inflicted by blunt instruments, apart from the youngest who died of a knife attack. In all surgeons estimation, the attacks were considered *'frenzied.'* Next witness, Michael Caine, who had heard about the attacks, reported the suspicious behaviour of a man he saw, around 12.15, washing his clothes in a pond, known as the figure of eight pit, in nearby Toxteth Park. The man had one leg of his trousers rolled up. Very interested, about 4.00 p.m. Police Constable Marks accompanied Caine to the scene where he discovered a letter containing Gleeson Wilson's details and bearing the address of 20 Leveson Street. He also found a bloodstained handkerchief.

The court then heard from a teenage boy, Edward McDermott, who said that about 9.30 on the morning of the murders Gleeson Wilson, wearing a hat with crepe tied around it, had given him a letter and, on the reward of three pennies asked him to deliver it to 20 Leveson St. This McDermott did. When he called to the home, the maid opened the door, called Gleeson Wilson and he took the letter from the boy. Intended for Mrs Hinrichson, the letter, the one found at the pond, was said to be a forged employer's reference for Gleeson Wilson thus ensuring his reliability and honesty. McDermott had also picked out Wilson at the identity parade.

Three cab drivers William Prescott, Thomas Jones and Robert Murray were next called. They claimed they saw Gleeson Wilson sweating and in an agitated state walking away from Leveson St. heading in the direction of Toxteth Park, they all found his behaviour suspicious. The three drivers noticed a distinctive hat with crepe band worn by the defendant. Oddly, he had one leg of his trousers rolled up. Cab driver Murray had also picked out Wilson at the identity parade.

George Moore, an assistant in Tunstall's Pawnbroker's London Road, told the court that at 12.35 a man he believed to be Gleeson Wilson attempted to pawn a watch. Moore said the man, wearing a hat with a crepe band, became agitated by his questions and left the shop. Moore thought the behaviour suspicious enough to report it to a policeman.

Joshua Finn informed the court that Gleeson Wilson came into his shop on Great Homer Street, about half a mile from London Road, at about 12.45 where he purchased a pair of trousers and changed into them. Finn said he wrapped the trousers Gleeson Wilson's removed and noticed blood on them below the knee. Finn returned them to his customer. The court heard then heard that outside the shop passer-by, Henry Worthington, received the trousers as a gift from Gleeson Wilson.

Gleeson Wilson was next in Great Howard St. at Jacob Samuel's barber shop where he asked for both a shave and a wig. He also wanted to know where he could purchase a ship's ticket for the USA. Samuel told him where he could buy a wig, but when he introduced him to people who could sell him a ticket to America, Gleeson Wilson fled.

Gleeson Wilson made his way to Tranmere, the court heard next, to spend the evening with his wife at her father's address. He returned by way of the ferry the following day. At around 3-4 p.m. he Gleeson Wilson turned up at his lodgings in where the landlady, Margaret Collopy told the court he borrowed a shirt. He once again tried to sell the watch for £6 this time at Israel Samuel's shop in Great Howard

Street. Samuel became suspicious and told his son to accompany Gleeson Wilson to a non-existent shop on Dale Street to obtain a receipt for the watch. The shop turned out to be a police station and Gleeson Wilson was arrested.

Defending barrister, James Pollock, spoke on behalf of Gleeson Wilson, but chose not to use his alibi, which had been discredited at the coroner's inquest. He instead began his address by accusing the police of coaching witnesses. It was impossible for Gleeson Wilson to be in all those places at the times given. For example, he could not have been in Toxteth Park at 12.15, then London Road at 12.35 and Great Homer Street at 12.45, a complicated journey of about two miles.

Pollock claimed the only real sightings of the perpetrator were by delivery boys Carney and McDermott. Carney, said Pollock, barely saw the man through a half open door and this for no more than a few seconds. A lot seemed to be made of Gleeson Wilson's clothing said Pollock. Several witnesses paid a lot of attention to his hat, which some of them did admit to seeing on a table outside the courtroom on the way in. (Gleeson Wilson was asked to wear the same hat in the identity parade). Cab driver Murray in particular asked him to put it on and was then able to swear absolutely Gleeson Wilson was the man he saw. Mary Parr also picked out Gleeson Wilson in the hospital by his headwear.

The watch was the incriminating evidence, said Pollock, and although it may well have belonged to Mrs Hinrichson there was no evidence to suggest that Gleeson Wilson stole it. If the motive for the murders was robbery, why was more jewellery not stolen and where was the rest of it? Why commit four horrific murders and then wander around the town trying to sell a watch for £6?

Pollock concluded that the people of Liverpool had prejudged Gleeson Wilson's guilt. The case had received huge publicity in the local press including lots of unfavourable reporting of Gleeson Wilson's background (his family back home in Ireland being described as *'feckless'* in the *Mercury*) and his violence towards his wife. Before the trial, Mary Parr's statement was printed in full in all local papers. although the judge, Mr Justice Pattison, did not allow for it to be submitted to the court.

Pollock never though questioned how both Gleeson Wilson's *'reference'* and bloodied handkerchief somehow managed to remain in the same place for more than four hours at the figure of eight pit. Why did he take them there? How did he come to leave them there?

Gleeson Wilson did not enter the witness box. The judge summed up and asked the jury to consider its verdict. Members did not feel it necessary to withdraw so remained where they sat and returned a guilty verdict inside three minutes. Gleeson Wilson was asked whether he had anything to say. He told the judge he was completely innocent and that he had been convicted for merely trying to sell a watch. He was subsequently sentenced to death by hanging at Kirkdale on 15th September.

Hundreds waited outside the court after the verdict. When Judge Pattison emerged around 9.00 pm he was clapped and many of the crowd continued to follow his carriage cheering it on the way. The *Mercury* referred to this as *'the revengeful spirit of human nature.'* In prison Gleeson Wilson continued to plead innocence. One of the priests attending him was said to be convinced by him. The *Mercury* had been campaigning for an end to the death penalty, but in the case of Gleeson Wilson declared, *'If ever there was a case in which the punishment of death could be tolerated – this was the one.'*

The evening before the execution, hundreds gathered at Kirkdale. Thousands travelled from all parts of Lancashire and Yorkshire to witness the event as train companies offered special rates of one shilling return to passengers. Over three hundred police officers were in attendance on the day itself to patrol a crowd estimated between 75,000 and 100,000. *'A carnival atmosphere,'* the Mercury reported:

> *'Young and old, rich and poor were seen to be wending their way to the sad spectacle. Mothers were leading their offspring by the hand and fathers were accompanying their daughters, brothers and sisters.'*

Food and beer were on sale. Thefts of watches and money were reported to the police.

At 12.00 noon and on the scaffold Gleeson Wilson was asked if he wanted to confess his guilt. He refused to do so. The country's chief executioner, William Calcraft was unwell and was replaced by 70-year-old Ben Howard of York, who proved to be completely incompetent. The drop was too short, and so was the white cap supposed to cover Gleeson Wilson's face which hardly reached over his eyebrows. As he dangled on the rope, those nearest the gallows saw his eyes bulge from their sockets and his face turn bright purple. Some fainted. Howard rushed forward to pull the cap down over Wilson's face. He was left hanging for another 15 minutes.

In extraordinary developments, a Professor Bally of Manchester was allowed to take a cast of Gleeson Wilson's skull. Bally, a well-known phrenologist, a person who studied the shape and protuberances of the skull, believed this would reveal the character and mental capacity of an of Gleeson Wilson. Bally later wrote that Gleeson Wilson's skull: *'displayed an utter absence of amiability and no taste for the beautiful.'* The condemned man, he concluded, was *'fox-like, cunning and obstinate.'*

Gleeson Wilson gained infamy across the country. An employee of *Madame Tussaud's Waxworks' Museum* in London was on hand to take away the clothing he wore at his execution and to acquire a waxwork impression of his skull. A Gleeson Wilson waxwork model was produced and remained on display at the museum for several years. Liverpool council, within a couple of years, changed the name of Leveson Street to Grenville Street.

* *

The administration of justice was often deemed unfair as in the case of John Roberts with the use of an approver to convict the poacher. Though Roberts eventually confessed to murder and four of his accomplices were transported, the approver lead poacher and gun carrier, Naaman Shaw, was not convicted of an offence, but was in fact rewarded for his part in the crime.

Gleeson Wilson, without doubt the prime suspect for the appalling Leveson Street murders, was guilty before he stepped foot in court. He was tried and convicted by the press and from there on his trial was a foregone conclusion. Mary Parr's statement was printed in full in all local papers and, although not allowed in evidence, it must have been very persuasive to anyone who read it.

Moreover, the way in which the police gathered evidence is very much open to question. For example, the set-up of the identity parades and Mary Parr's identification (Gleeson Wilson was always asked to wear a hat) were of dubious nature; the letter and handkerchief discovered at a location some four hours after they were left/dropped there: the witnesses' timings (it was impossible for all those who gave evidence to have seen him on the day); the witnesses who saw drops of blood on his trousers (the horrific nature of the murders would have left more than a few drops); all leave questions regarding police conduct in the prosecution of their case against Gleeson Wilson.

Infanticide

An unwanted pregnancy often brought misery and turmoil to many single women in Victorian Britain. A child born outside wedlock was regarded as *'illegitimate'*, without full legal status, a serious stigma in the nineteenth century. Charles Dickens' 1834 novel *Oliver Twist* opens with the title character's unmarried, pregnant mother, having been forced to enter the workhouse, about to give birth. A pregnancy before marriage was regarded as a source of ignominy for a woman in the early Victorian era. Accordingly, in the novel, Oliver's mother leaves home so as not to bring shame upon them.

A single woman in such a condition would, more often than not, find themselves ostracised by family and friends, and forced to leave home. For a great number of young working class women, live-in domestic service was the only form of employment and there are numerous examples of many such employees becoming pregnant and finding themselves banished from the household.

In anguish and shame, after giving birth, young, unmarried mothers frequently placed their infants in workhouses or simply abandoned them. Historian, Professor Hilary Marland (*Dangerous Motherhood: Insanity and Childbirth in Victorian Britain* 2004) says that the police in mid-Victorian Britain: *'thought no more of finding the dead body of a child in the street, than picking up a dead dog or cat.'*

The discovery of abandoned new-born babies was a regular occurrence in 1840s Liverpool. For instance, on 23 October 1846 the *Liverpool Mail* wrote of *'a man on his way to work found the body of a newly-born child floating in a water filled pit in Kirkdale'*. The authorities rarely attempted to track down mothers, and there is no evidence to suggest they did so in this case.

Some of the children found dead and abandoned were the victims of unnatural deaths and many of the mothers, if discovered, faced the full consequences of the law. At an inquest into the suspicious death of a new-born child in October 1847, Liverpool Borough Coroner, Philip Finch Curry, expressed his concern of such cases coming regularly before his court. Reported in the *Liverpool Mercury* on the 26th, he said he had heard from an:

> *'...eminent medical man that upwards of 20,000 children a year* (in Britain) *are annually murdered and the numbers in Liverpool are on the increase.'*

The coroner did not produce any evidence to substantiate his figures. If the evidence revealed a child had died as a consequence of violence, then an inquest jury would invariably return a verdict of *'wilful murder,'* but it was often accompanied by *'persons unknown.'* In one such case, the body of a new-born was discovered in Bittern Street, near London Road on 13 June 1848. The doctor told the coroner that the child had died because of *'external violence'*; the jury returned a verdict of *'wilful murder by persons unknown,' and* no one was charged with the crime.

From time to time, inquest juries returned verdicts of murder and named the alleged perpetrator. Many women therefore found themselves in court charged with murder and an additional charge (or more often than not an alternative charge) of *concealing a birth.'* In court, many of the women's stories follow a similar pattern. When their pregnancy was discovered, they were often ostracised and cast out by family and friends. Consequently, many incredibly gave birth alone, sometimes in dreadful circumstances such as in alleyways or empty houses.

At the trial of Mary Green, 25 of Circus Street, near the town centre, the *Mercury* reported on 2 April 1847 that her husband had been *'away for several years.'* An un-named witness and friend said she had spoken to Mary to ask her if she was pregnant. Green denied it. The witness added that a few weeks later she saw Mary carrying *'a bundle'* to nearby Springfield Street only to return shortly afterwards empty handed.

Suspicious, the witness went to check and in a back entry discovered the body of a new-born wrapped and hidden. She informed the police, who in turn called in a surgeon, George Woods, to examine the child. In the surgeon's opinion, the child was alive at birth, but, unable to find evidence of external injuries, could not therefore fully determine the cause of death. The jury returned a verdict of not guilty on the murder, charge but a guilty verdict of concealment on Mary Green. She was sentenced to three months' hard labour.

Servant, Elizabeth Russell aged 28, appeared in court charged with murder and concealment of a birth. At the time of her court appearance, in August 1842, Russell had been in service to a Mrs Cole of Sandon Street (near Upper Parliament Street) for seven years. Reporting the case, the *Mercury* said Cole told the court that on 9 June, Russell went to bed early saying she was unwell. Next morning Cole discovered a baby wrapped in a blanket in the midden. She then questioned Russell who at first denied any knowledge of the baby, but within hours admitted to having given birth.

The new-born was examined by three separate surgeons. Giving evidence to the court, the first, Thomas Blackburn, said the baby boy was alive at birth and his death was due to the insertion of a sharp instrument in the brain. Blackburn's evidence was corroborated by fellow surgeons Edward Batty and Benjamin Brown.

Defence attorney, Charles Wilkins, claimed that the surgeons hastily reached their conclusions. He asserted that Elizabeth had tried to cover the boy's head which led to an accidental injury to the baby. Wilkins added that Elizabeth then panicked and hid her baby's body in the midden. In mitigation, Wilkins argued that *'Elizabeth had worked hard at her job and was of good character.'* In fact, he added, Elizabeth was a victim of seduction, though he failed to mention by whom.

Following the judge's summing up, the all male jury retired to consider its verdicts. Debating for what was a relatively lengthy period of a half hour, it returned verdicts of not guilty of murder, but guilty of concealment. The judge on passing sentence told Russell that she had *'neglected her duty of care for a newborn child'* and for this she should be punished. He sentenced her to two years' hard labour at Kirkdale.

In 1846, 21-year-old Mary Baxter, a lodger living in Edge Hill, was also charged with murder and concealment. The *Liverpool Mail* reported that Mary's landlady told the court that on 28 October Mary *'went to bed early saying she felt unwell.'* The landlady told the court that Mary had, after she was asked, denied being pregnant.

Calling on Mary the following morning, Mary, the landlady said, appeared to be in a poor state of health, so a doctor was called. Under examination, Mary confessed to giving birth and hiding her baby in the privy. There, the body of the child was discovered with an *'apron string around its neck'*.

An additional medical man, James Barton-Nottage was called to examine the child. In his opinion, the child was alive at birth and it had died as a result of deliberate strangulation, but under cross examination, he was less certain. Unconvinced by Barton-Nottage's evidence, the judge directed the jury to acquit Baxter of murder, but to consider a verdict of concealment. The jury found her guilty of the secondary charge and Mary was sentenced to two years' imprisonment with hard labour.

* *

On 26 October 1847, the *Mercury* reported from the Coroner's Court on the case of 19-year-old Jane Charnock, a domestic servant of seven weeks to Mary Ann Walmsley, Upper Pitt Street, Toxteth. On 11 October, Jane complained of a headache and retired to bed early. The householder and other servants suspected that Jane was pregnant when she joined the staff. The following morning, a concerned Mrs Walmesley who believed Jane had given birth sent for a doctor. Having been supplied with the suspicions, the doctor put this to Jane, who admitted to giving birth a few hours earlier. She had hidden the child in a cradle under her bed. The doctor examined the new-born and concluded that it had died because of strangulation.

The inquest jury, following advice from the coroner, Philip Finch Curry returned a verdict of wilful murder. In December 1847, Jane Charnock, charged with murder and concealment, appeared at the Assize Court. Several witnesses told the court that the defendant appeared pregnant upon arrival at the Walmesley home, but Jane told them she was overweight and needed to wear a *'stay'* (a strip of bone or metal used to stiffen part of a garment such as a corset). On the evening before giving birth, Jane appeared unwell. She went to bed in a room she shared with two of Mrs Walmesley's children (ages not recorded). The two children heard nothing.

The following morning, Mrs Walmesley called in on Jane and discovered there were no bedclothes in the room and asked whether she had given birth and murdered her child. Jane replied no to both questions. In deceit, Walmesley told Jane she looked and required treatment, so she called for a doctor in order to elicit a confession, which proved successful. The doctor informed the court that in his opinion the baby had been suffocated by the stays which formed part of the wrapping used to prevent discovery of the child.

Defence barrister, Mr James, told the court that Jane had indeed wrapped the baby to conceal its discovery, but, because she had inadvertently done so in such a vigorous manner, it accidently caused the death of the baby. Accepting the defence argument, the jury found Jane not guilty of murder, but guilty of concealment. She was sentenced to 12 months' imprisonment with hard labour.
On the same day, two other women, similarly charged received similar sentences to Jane having both been declared not guilty of murder, but guilty of concealment.

An almost incidental piece of information was disclosed at the trial of Jane Charnock. The court heard that prior to working for Mary Ann Walmesley, Jane had worked in service for the Earl of Balcarres, a title created in Scotland in 1651 for Alexander Lindsay. The Balcarres family eventually moved to Lancashire where it became owners of coalmines in the county. In 1840, the then earl, James Lindsay, opened Haigh Hall, part of a huge 500-acre country estate near Wigan. Though not fully disclosed, it would appear that Jane was employed as a servant at the hall. Jane left service in Haigh Hall in August 1847.

Illustrating many of the prevailing Victorian attitudes towards young, single pregnant women, Jane's treatment begs some intriguing questions. Why did a seven-month pregnant 19-year-old woman leave (or was sent from) a stately home? Census records show her parents alive at the time with her father, Thomas, working as a coalminer, presumably in an Earl of Balcarres owned colliery. Who was the father of Jane's baby, a member of the Balcarres family or a fellow servant perhaps? Was the family embarrassed and ashamed by Jane's pregnancy, therefore despatching her to Liverpool?

Whatever the answers to these questions, within four months of leaving Wigan, Jane Charnock, although cleared of murder, was serving hard labour in Kirkdale Prison. The 1851 census, records a 23-year-old Jane Charnock working as *'power loon tenter'* (a repairer of power looms) in Haigh (close to Wigan) Lancashire.

In Jane's, and for that matter all the above cases, a possible father was never mentioned or asked for at the trials. Mid-Victorian juries however, in Liverpool anyway, appear to have been very reluctant to find the great majority of the women guilty of murder. If found guilty of murder, juries could not be certain that the women before them would be reprieved. Thus, aware that the women would have been sentenced to death, a guilty verdict of concealment was therefore probably an acceptable alternative.

The Case of Catherine Comerford

A charge of murder and concealment against 23-year-old Catherine Comerford went beyond the Liverpool court. The case brought into conflict two huge Victorian institutions, the court and the board responsible for overseeing the workhouse, the select vestry and their individual representatives, the chief magistrate and workhouse governor.

On Friday 9 October 1846, living in a brothel in Hart Street off London Road, Catherine Comerford, feeling unwell. went to bed early. The following morning, owner of the premises, Ellen Darby, called on Catherine only to discover the dead body of a new-born child under the bedclothes. Catherine admitted to giving birth and apologised for not informing Mrs Darby of her situation. The nearby workhouse surgeon was called and following examination he concluded that the child had been suffocated. Two more doctors were called to examine the baby's body.

At the coroner's inquest a few days later, Catherine denied murdering her child. The latter doctors told the inquest that they could not determine the cause of death saying it was possible the baby was stillborn, but they also admitted to the possibility of suffocation. All three doctors agreed that there were no signs of physical violence. Coroner Finch Curry, concluded that the child died of *'want and proper attention'* and that it would be inappropriate to return a verdict of murder or manslaughter. Taking advice from the coroner, the jury returned a verdict of stillborn. Catherine, however, would still have to face the court on a charge of concealment and was remanded to prison to await trial in a week's time. However, which was far from unusual, there were no spaces in local prisons at the time. Catherine instead was remanded to the workhouse.

At her appearance before magistrate, Edward Rushton, Catherine told the court that on the Wednesday prior to the birth she had gone, out of desperation, to the workhouse. There she was examined by the workhouse surgeon and was told that she was not yet ready to give birth. Catherine was turned out the following morning and, without alternative accommodation, made her way to the Hart Street brothel.

The workhouse surgeon confirmed her version of events. The next witness called, however, sent the whole case in a totally new direction.

Police officer, John Owens, assigned to look after Catherine at the workhouse, said that as the two were preparing to make their way from the workhouse it began to rain heavily. Owens said that the prisoner appeared to be very weak and he believed she would have difficulty in making the journey on foot, a distance of about one mile. Calling on the assistance of the workhouse governor, David Evans, Owens asked if a cart could be commandeered to transport Comerford to the court. The governor replied saying that workhouse carts were not used for this type of journey and: *'if this bad woman is guilty of murder she should be executed.'*

Officer Owens told the court that the governor was prone to speak in such a manner. Accepting Owens' statement, an angry Rushton immediately adjourned the case and sent instructions for Evans to attend the court. Catherine Comerford, he declared, was not before him on a murder charge. The developments led the *Mercury, Mail* and other local papers to take an exceptional interest in Catherine's case, reporting on the meetings of the Select Vestry and magistrates' meetings.

Over the following days, Governor Evans sent messages to Rushton saying he was too unwell to make his appearance in court. Meanwhile, the Select Vestry debated whether or not he should attend the court. It ultimately concluded that he should, but it too sent a message to Rushton saying that the magistrate's behaviour towards the governor was very unacceptable. Officer Owens' statement to the court had also angered the Select Vestry. After taking evidence from nursing staff, who claimed that Owens would sit on female prisoners' beds and talk to them, the committee resolved not to allow police officers further entry to the workhouse to guard remanded prisoners. The Select Vestry also noted in its minutes that Catherine Comerford was *'a woman of the town who had concealed the birth of a bastard child.'*

Eventually attending the court, Evans informed Rushton that the words attributed to him were a *'mixture of truth and falsehood.'* The governor claimed he simply said that if the prisoner were guilty of a crime such as murder, *'she ought to suffer the laws of the country.'* Rushton, however, chose to accept Officer Owens' version. Rushton, rebuking Governor Evans, informed him that, *'...in this country a person is innocent until proven guilty.'* He added that Comerford had every right to be taken care of and concluded:

> *'...it did not become any public official, not least the governor of the workhouse, to make use of such language to a person in her condition that would further distress her.'*

The magistrate's treatment of Governor Evans further angered the Select Vestry. A resolution, passed at its next meeting and forwarded to Rushton, stated that:

> *'Magistrates should not reprove the workhouse staff or express an opinion before an issue has been dealt with by the Select Vestry. In ordering the governor to the court and rebuking him for his words and actions Rushton had held the governor up for public ridicule.'*

The Select Vestry's resolution led to an extraordinary magistrates' meeting chaired by Mayor George Hall Lawrence with, amongst others, William Rathbone in attendance. Rushton, asking for his words to be put on record, stated that he believed that he was indeed within his right to reprove the actions of the workhouse staff if it was, in his opinion, right to do so in the administration of the law.

Rushton followed up with a statement from Catherine Comerford. She informed the magistrate, that she had come to Liverpool from Ireland twelve months earlier and taken work as a domestic servant of a Mrs Dawson of Crown Street. A few months later she discovered she was pregnant, the father, Mrs Dawson's un-named brother. When the pregnancy became clear Mrs Dawson dismissed her.

Over the following weeks, she stayed at various lodging houses, but quickly spent the little money she had and was forced to pawn all her possessions. Standing in the only garments she possessed Catherine applied to the parish for relief, where she was given an order to attend the workhouse. On her second day, she was examined by the workhouse surgeon, with the governor present, and was informed that the birth was *'still some way off.'*

Turned out of the workhouse, Catherine made her way to the brothel, a few hundred yards away in Hart Street, where she was employed as a servant. Ten days later she gave birth to her child. After the statement, the other 16 magistrates gave to give Rushton a vote of confidence and their full support, which it passed on the Select Vestry.

The spat between the two institutions effectively concluded at the next Select Vestry meeting. It resolved not to discuss the issue any further, but not before stating that it did not trust Officer Owens and it was erroneous for Rushton to accept his word over that of the governor. There is no record of the committee discussing Catherine Comerford's statement presented by Rushton or apologising for labelling her *'a woman of the street'*.

Finally, what of Catherine herself? She originally went back to work for Mrs Dawson. The 1851 census identifies her living in Mount Pleasant. On Christmas Day 1852 she married Richard Sefton in nearby St Nicholas Church and in 1854 she gave birth to a daughter which the couple named Catherine. Richard died in September 1857. The 1861 census documents the two Catherines still living in Mount Pleasant. There is no record of either of them in the 1871 Liverpool census.

* *

One final story concerning the birth of children in unpleasant surroundings, does have something of a happier ending. On 23 November 1843, the *Mercury* reported that a police officer on patrol in Frederick Street, Toxteth came across a young woman giving birth in an entry. He called for assistance and him and a nearby householder helped with the birth. Incredibly the young woman produced twins and all three were taken to the Southern Hospital to receive medical attention.

The *Mercury* learned that the married woman was working in domestic service, but six months earlier her husband, a sailor, had returned to sea. When learning of her pregnancy the householders turned her out leaving her, she said, *'entirely destitute.'* Having nowhere to turn, she slept rough and fearing condemnation was forced to give birth alone. Two months on, the paper reported that mother and children were doing well.

5. Black '47': Liverpool and the Great Irish Famine

In 1997 Liverpool played host to a series of events commemorating the 150th anniversary of the Great Irish Famine. In Ireland, 1847 earned the horrific soubriquet *'Black '47,'* as a consequence of the huge scale of death that year and the ensuing massive migration of citizens of whom almost 300,000 arrived in Liverpool. Suffering from the effects of famine, cholera and typhus, around 7,000 were eventually to die in the town.

The Great Famine Commemoration Committee of Liverpool, formed in the early 1990s, organised and oversaw a series of events, not only to honour the memory of those who died, but also to celebrate Irish historical contributions to the city. The committee installed a series of plaques at various famine sites around the city, the most prominent of which are situated at Clarence Dock and St. Luke's Church on Lecce Street. The later was unveiled by the then Irish President, Mary Robinson.

Memorial church services, art installations, educational initiatives, public lectures and radio documentaries dedicated to recollecting the Famine experience in Liverpool, were also part of the commemorations. Visitors and locals also took part in guided tours on the *Irish Great Hunger Heritage Trail*.

Why is Liverpool then integral to this important period in Ireland's history?

* *

On the eve of the famine, the potato was the main food source for around half of Ireland's population. Over three million peasant farmers and labourers relied almost exclusively on the crop for sustenance, so when the famine struck, the poorest people in the potato dependent areas of the south and west of Ireland were most devastated. The famine began with the appearance of a new, devastating potato blight in 1845. The fungus, *'phytophthora infestans'*, entered European ports aboard ships carrying potatoes from the American continent and was spread rapidly by wind and water-borne spores during the late summer and autumn of 1845.

Though effecting many parts of Western Europe, nowhere suffered more distress than Ireland, such was the dependence on a single crop. The fungus destroyed one-third of the 1845 harvest, a severe shortfall, but one that was endured without mass starvation. However, when the blight returned it did so with far greater vengeance the following summer, turning almost the entire crop to pulp. The consequences were catastrophic. Without sufficient land or time to plant an alternative crop and an adequate income, Ireland's poorer farmers were soon desperate for food. Many were driven to eat anything that might offer nourishment: grass, leaves, seaweed, rotten potatoes or rancid meat.

At the time of the famine, Ireland was part of the British Isles and therefore the Westminster government was ultimately responsibility for the country's citizens. The British government initially established food depots in each county from which imported American maize was sold cheaply to lower food prices and stave off hunger. Many citizens though were destitute and could not afford the food.

There was no shortage of food in Ireland, but laissez-faire, the reigning economic orthodoxy of the day, held that the government should not interfere in economic affairs. Stopping the export of Irish food to feed the starving, was an unacceptable policy. Consequently, thousands of fleeing, starving famine victims were often forced to travel across the Irish Sea from Dublin, Cork and Belfast to Liverpool in ships crammed with tons of food, such as beef, mutton, ham and dairy produce.

The British government didn't see itself as a charitable institution, distributing food for free, so introduced public work schemes, employing the hungry in return for a day's food. People working on the schemes were employed, for example, on building walls and repairing roads that went nowhere. However, the schemes, which employed and therefore fed 700,000 people, fell far short of offering complete relief. Most people working were extremely weak from hunger and incapable of completing their tasks satisfactorily. The schemes were eventually abandoned as costly and ineffective.

Many Irish citizens believed government ministers and officials were hard-hearted and cruel. Assistant secretary to the Treasury and director of government relief in prime minister's Sir John Russell's administration Sir Charles Edward Trevelyan confirmed their beliefs. Trevelyan interpreted the potato blight as the subject of divine deliverance. In his 1848 book, *The Irish Crisis*, he claimed that God had wrought famine as a remedy to over-population.

It was Trevelyan's decision to close the public work schemes. He believed responsibility for feeding the starving Irish should be borne by the Irish ratepayers. The government's Soup Kitchen Act of 1847 called for the food to be provided through taxes collected by local relief committees from Irish landowners and merchants. When in operation, most ratepayers were opposed to the policy and were unwilling to bear the expense of mounting poor rates. They believed that if you gave the hungry soup daily they would return ad infinitum. One solution therefore, as Major Denis Mahon had done (see Chapter One, Port and Docks) was to pay the shipping costs of the starving to emigrate to ports such as Liverpool. A one-off fare across the Irish Sea would be more cost effective than subsidising a hungry population.

By summer of 1847, tens of thousands of desperate, diseased and starving emigrants had boarded Liverpool bound merchant ships, not passenger ships. Goods and livestock had first claim in the vessels. The famine victims were added later and their situation would often worsen before it got better. In all kinds of weather, the great majority travelled on the open deck of a steamer, on a journey of 22 to 36 hours from Cork or 14 to 28 hours from Dublin.

No amenities for the passengers well being were provided. They were, packed shoulder-to-shoulder, unable to get food or drink, drenched with spray. The overcrowded conditions aboard ship meant that many passengers, if they were not already carrying diseases such as typhus, were vulnerable to infection. Very few would have ever travelled at sea and many of them were therefore seasick.
In 1848 a House of Lords enquiry into conditions aboard the Irish ships heard that:

> 'Upon arrival in Liverpool the people were positively prostrated, and scarcely able to walk after they got out of the steamers...The manner in which passengers are conveyed from Irish to English ports is disgraceful, dangerous and inhuman.'

Many emigrants died as soon as they landed on the Liverpool shore.

* *

Liverpool received thousands of victims fleeing the horrors of the famine before 1847. The priority for victims was food and survival. A significant number arrived through the first nine or ten months of 1846, but the figures increased dramatically toward the end of the year. In the week ending Christmas Day 1846 with the workhouse full, Liverpool Select Vestry reported that 4,490 Irish families had been provided with outdoor relief in the form of soup and bread. Within a couple of weeks, the number of starving victims landing at the port of Liverpool began to rise steadily.

At its first 1847 meeting, held on 12 January, the Vestry published the numbers of people applying for parish relief. On Monday 4th soup and bread were distributed to 3,189; on Thursday 7th to 4,692 and on Saturday 9th to 8,362. In total over six days 29,417 people applied for parish relief. The figures alarmed the Liverpool press. Many newspapers demanded the government and other parts of the country not leave Liverpool with the sole responsibility for the well-being of the new arrivals. The *Liverpool Mercury* on 15 January claimed the situation was *'grossly unfair'* and the burden should be shared with the rest of the country. It stated:

> *'The number of starving Irish daily landed in our quays is appalling and the parish of Liverpool has at present the painful and most costly task of keeping them alive... Liverpool at the moment is bearing a burden, which belongs neither to itself, the county or England, but the whole of the UK.'*

The paper suggested ratepayers should:

> *'Exert themselves diligently to seek redress at the hands of parliament. Petitions ought to be addressed to both houses (of*

Parliament) *praying that the extraordinary circumstances of the present alarming crisis may be met by extraordinary means.'*

The Select Vestry applied to the government for assistance. The response of the Home Secretary, Sir George Grey, was printed in the *Mercury* on 22 January:

'I am not aware of any means by which Her Majesty's Government could prevent the Irish poor coming to Liverpool and the existence of any funds applicable to the repayment of the parish of Liverpool the amount of extraordinary expenses incurred.'

Without government aid, members of the vestry debated how they could reduce the numbers applying for assistance and thereby reduce the bill to the ratepayers (the rate in 1847 was eventually to double from two to four shillings). James Stitt informed the meeting that he was aware of Glasgow Parish putting paupers back on ships and returning them to Ireland. Whilst William Johnson added that the parish ought to send the paupers back once they had received relief.

James Austin reminded members that the removal of paupers would require an appearance at the Magistrate's Court. The current law required the courts to act against individuals, which would be a lengthy and expensive process. Only an amendment to the law would allow speedy removal. Samuel Seward then suggested that as *'There are many towns between Liverpool and London, the distressed poor could be sent off to them by train.'* The Vestry Chairman, Reverend Augustus Campbell, said this was virtually impossible, adding that he believed members could do little but talk. He therefore suggested, through petition signed by the townsfolk, appealing again to the government soon.

* *

Defrauding the parish was a major concern of the Select Vestry which spent a great deal of its time listening to accounts of perceived fraud. On 27 January, a letter from police Head Constable James Dowling was relayed to the board. Dowling wrote that one of his officers had witnessed a woman of four children receiving soup tickets even though he had *'seen her begging in Kirkdale Road with a barefoot child'*. The officer informed Dowling that he *'saw the woman the same afternoon half a mile away begging in Penrhyn Street.'* The Select Vestry declared those who apply for parish relief and beg be charged with receiving money by deception.

The Chairman reported a story told to him by two female acquaintances. His acquaintances, he said, heard two Irishwomen talking in the street and one asked the other *'How do you get on?* The reply was *'Oh grandly. I sent £2 to the Dublin Savings Bank yesterday.'* These words were scarcely uttered when a gentleman passed by and the woman dropped to her knees and *'begged for the love of God'* that he would give her something to prevent her and her two children from starving.

Committee member, John Mellor, said he had heard that the Bold Street post office was *'besieged by Irish sending money orders over to their friends'.* Senior Reverend Jonathan Brooks feared that the generous nature of the parish was encouraging the Irish to come to Liverpool, stating:

> *'The persons who applied at the office got twelve ounces of bread and two pints of soup and therefore they were better off here than they were in Ireland.'*

The board believed that locals too were taking advantage of Liverpool's *'generous nature'* as more tales of alleged deception were heard, including one of a local woman applying for relief for her and her large family saying her husband was out of work. The board however discovered that her husband was working for a Liverpool gas company. A similar story was heard of a '...*woman claiming for her and her four children as a result of her husband deserting the family and leaving them destitute'*. The woman's husband was *'discovered working in Toxteth Park earning £2 per week.'*

Undoubtedly, there was evidence of begging and it would be a fair assumption to make that some people may have taken advantage of a system distributing *'free'* food. The Select Vestry was nevertheless prepared to amend policy which would affect thousands partly based on anecdotal, circumstantial evidence.

The board also believed that there were more Irish children applying for relief than were actually arriving in the town. So rather than feeding people who simply applied for relief at a soup kitchen, the Select Vestry employed relieving officers to visit parts of Liverpool dispensing *'soup tickets'* to those deemed in dire need. The tickets would then be brought to the soup kitchen and food dispensed to the holder. The new system certainly appeared to work, as the parish figures indicate. On 1 February, with an open system, more than 22,000 received food; however, on the 2nd, with a ticket system in operation, the number dramatically reduced to less than 5,000.

The numbers suggest that the vestry's suspicions of deception were well founded. However, were relieving officers really able to reach all those in need? Knowing the priority of the Select Vestry, the reduction in costs, did relieving officers want to find all those in need? Furthermore historian, Frank Neal, (*Black '47: Britain and the*

Famine Irish: 1998) claims: *'Many Irish were scared of applying because they thought they ran the risk of being sent back to Ireland.'*

* *

On 1 January 1847 Dr William Henry Duncan was appointed Liverpool's Medical Officer of Health. One of his roles was to identify and prevent the spread of infectious diseases, but his task was to quickly become enormous. Duncan believed that overcrowded, insanitary caused diseases, such as cholera and typhus, and helped spread the disease. The worst properties were cleared of residents and condemned, but by early 1847, had yet to be demolished. The starving, disease infected arriving Irish discovered the condemned housing, ripped boards from the covered windows and doors and took up occupancy. Duncan toured the districts in the early 1847 Duncan and later reported to the council:

> *'Irish paupers, driven from their miserable cabins by fear of starvation, were landing in Liverpool in unusual numbers. In February I stated that in one densely populated district between Scotland Road and Vauxhall Road fever has become more than usually prevalent that more than one half of the whole deaths from it had taken place in this Irish district.'*

Duncan, in his medical report for 1847 wrote that the Irish were largely responsible for turning Liverpool into *'A city of the Plague'*. Irish famine victims became so associated with typhus that the disease became known as the *'Irish fever.'*

Typhus fever, discovered by an American scientist Howard Taylor Ricketts in 1910, is caused by microscopic bacteria and spread by lice. The lice would acquire bacteria by feeding on the blood of an infected person. A very infectious disease, it makes its way into the human body in various ways, for example via a bite from an infected louse; any contact with infected louse excrement or its bodily fluids, such as a scratch or injury in the skin: lastly through airborne dried louse excrement entering the body via the eyes or nose.

A combination of poor housing and the movement of large numbers through the port, made Liverpool particularly vulnerable to typhus. The surviving Irish who crammed into the filthy condemned housing and cellars as well as overcrowded lodging houses, only helped the disease thrive. On 8 March the Select Vestry were informed of typhus killing eight people in Crosbie Street and four children dying of the disease in St. Martin Street. On 13 March the *Liverpool Journal* in a report headlined *'A Skibbereen in Liverpool'* (Skibbereen referred to one of the worst affected towns in Ireland) wrote:

> *'We fear that at this moment suffering is as great and undeserved in this town as can be witnessed, even on the west coast of Ireland. Two or three cases in one court have come to our knowledge. That court is Webster's Court in Oriel Street...Last week a whole family was down with fever, there was no nurse, no doctor. An infant died and the mother was only able to push the dead body off the straw in which she was herself was dying.'*

The first of ten Catholic priests, Father Peter Nightingale aged 32 of St. Anthony's Church, died as a consequence of contracting typhus during a visit to Oriel Street.

On 12 March the *Mercury*, concerned with the rising incidence of the disease, appealed *'...for sheds to be constructed in all parts of the town.'* Duncan, aiming to control the disease, recommended the commissioning of such *'fever sheds.'* He further told the council and the Select Vestry on 23 March, that: *'...the health of the town would not be improved unless the Irish could be removed.'*

The council and Select Vestry agreed on the necessity of fever sheds and sites were identified including in the north at Great Homer Street and in the south on Brownlow Hill. On other site identified was a guano warehouse (guano: the excrement of seabirds used as a fertiliser) in Great Howard Street, belonged to Select Vestry board member William Earle. The vestry, responsible for funding the fever sheds, agreed to pay Earle £900 per year for the use of his warehouse. The guano was in the warehouse when the first typhus victims moved in. At an April meeting of the Vestry, Earle informed the committee that the *'guano was in the process of being removed.'* There is no record stating that this ever happened.

The authorities were finding it increasingly difficult to deal with the rising fatalities. Grave diggers at St. Mary's Cemetery, situated on the corner of Mulberry Street and Cambridge Street (which is now part of Liverpool University campus), found themselves overwhelmed by the numbers of deceased. The *Mercury* reported on Friday 23 April that grave diggers *'arrived to find 16 coffins outside the gates and a similar number of bodies thrown over the walls of the cemetery.'*

The specially built fever sheds on Brownlow Hill, close to Liverpool Workhouse, caused great consternation amongst local residents. The *Mercury* received dozens of letters from residents who threatened to leave their homes for fear of contagion. Some suggested that the sheds be built away from the town in less populated areas such as Aigburth or Allerton. The council received desperate appeals, but Duncan informed the Select Vestry by letter on 15 May that residents need not be alarmed as the sheds would be well ventilated, *'...their fears are purely imaginary'* Still the protests continued and once more Duncan was impelled to respond, this time in a letter to the council on 8 June. He wrote that he had examined the sheds and in his opinion:

> '...no danger is to be apprehended to the health of the inhabitants of the neighbourhood from the sheds in question. Theory and experience alike justify me in giving this opinion in the most decided terms. No instance is on record, as far as I am aware, of the contagion of typhus being propagated under such circumstances.'

Typhus was now officially classified an epidemic. In late March the disease caused the deaths of 25 to 30 people. In the final week of May, it had killed 150 and in the third week of June, 215. The summer was expected to see a further increase in the numbers dying.

On 12 May, at a mass town meeting, which included members of the Select Vestry, council and magistrate's court, discussed options to tackle the growing numbers of Irish immigrants and the spread of fever. Reporting from a very angry meeting, the *Mercury*, wrote of several people attacking the Irish for coming to Liverpool to *'feed and beg from the hard-working people of the town.'* Irish people were accused of being *'criminal, lazy and unwilling to work.'*

Having returned from a four-week tour of Ireland and seeing for himself the devastating effects of the famine in the country, William Rathbone argued to the contrary. He told the meeting that he heard:

> '...the dying groans of people' and saw desperate and willing people 'walking with spades over their shoulders looking for work but unable to find any. It's up to the government to get it right... The Irish landlords are abusing their power, not giving work and

removing people from their homes... The landlords should be compelled to find work or offer relief.'

Rathbone was not surprised that people chose to leave Ireland for towns such as Liverpool.

The meeting resolved to further petition parliament and recommended unanimously that the mayor, George Hall Lawrence, request both houses of parliament on behalf of the petitioners, to *'Amend the laws on the removal of poor persons of England and to make further relief for the paupers of Ireland.'*

Armed with the signed petition, on 17 June, a deputation of nine Liverpool townsmen consisting of members of the Select Vestry and council, as well as Dr Duncan and borough magistrate Edward Rushton, met the Home Secretary, Sir George Grey. On 23 June, the government responded to Liverpool's appeal with an amendment to the *Poor Law Removal Act*. The act gave Liverpool special powers to remove in bulk *'Irish-born paupers who did not have official approval for settlement in England.'* Parish officials met with Irish shipping agents to make plans for the return of Irish migrants.

Though entirely satisfactory for the Select Vestry, the change of law change did not prevent the committee from receiving criticism. A surgeon, W.T. Callon of Islington Terrace, wrote to the *Mercury* on 6 July accusing the vestry of apathy in the face of the epidemic. He charged members of the board with *'spending time debating issues'* and failing to respond to the danger of typhus.

Callon wrote of a case in which *'a Samaritan friend'* of his discovered a *'...six-month pregnant woman lying in a miserable cellar in Hornby Street* (Vauxhall) *in a state of fever.'* She asked to be removed to a fever shed, but was refused, being told there were no places. The woman died shortly afterwards. Callon added that: *the dead woman's blackened corpse lay on a filthy bed of straw for two more days with no sign of it being removed.* The woman's body was still in place when he penned the letter to the newspaper. 'Public, draw your own conclusions,' was his parting critical comment on the work of the Select Vestry.

At its 20 July meeting, the secretary to the Select Vestry informed members that:

> 'There was a great decrease in the amount of the money expended on behalf of the Irish poor and their numbers are diminishing. Many were going back to Ireland or going to the country.'

Meanwhile four fever ships, known as lazarettos, *Akbar, Druid, Newcastle* and *Lavinia* were anchored on the Mersey to counteract and contain the rising number of typhus cases. Within two weeks, Captain Willcocks of the *Akbar* died of the disease. From the viewpoint of the vestry, the system of identifying and removing fever victims and pauper Irish was working well. The vestry had obtained two 'cars' to collect fever victims from their homes to transport them to the sheds. If medical officers deemed patients well enough, they could then be returned to Ireland.

Also on 20 July, in a letter to fellow brethren, DB Tidmarsh of Downside Abbey, a religious monastery in Somerset. newly arrived Catholic priest, Father Gregory Lane, wrote of his experience in Liverpool (*Downside Review: Volume 29, 1910*). Lane had been in the town just a few weeks, spending a short time at St. Anthony's, Scotland Road, when he was transferred to St. Mary's Edmund Street (near Tithebarn Street). Lane told Tidmarsh of the death of a fellow priest, whose name he could not recall (it was likely to be Father William Vincent Dale who died of typhus on 26 June). Lane said he stayed with the priest for a few days during his and Lane and was with him when he died. In a graphic description, he wrote: '...*soon after he expired, 'the poor man's stomach exploded.'*

Lane wrote of his time touring the town visiting homes and fever sheds. In one, likely to be the Great Howard guano warehouse, he met and spoke to several patients, one of whom asked if the priest would hear her confession. He promised to do so, the following day, but on his return to the shed, the woman had died.

Walking on one street he *'came across a boy of about four years lying in the street who said "someone is sick in that house".'* He entered and discovered a girl of *'about 15 years of age lying on a bed of straw, ill with fever.'* The girl told Lane that her mother and father had both died in the bed, but both wished to speak to a minister of religion, something they were unable to achieve. He was able to have the girl removed to a fever shed. He wrote that he would take time to call on the girl's siblings to check on their health. Father Lane's letter is a description of despair and helplessness.

Into August and the numbers of Irish removed was increasing. On the 12th, the Select Vestry said that between 400-450 Irish paupers per week were being shipped out. William Earle told the meeting that day that many removed had been evicted from condemned houses. To *'much laughter'*, Earle said that several of those evicted *'...claimed they were born in this town, but when asked in which street they were born they were unable to answer.'* When Irish pauperism was an agenda item, Earle often raised a laugh with sarcastic comments.

It was, though now Ireland's turn to complain about Liverpool's policy. Reported in the *Liverpool Courier* of 25 August, a Dublin registrar protested that most of the arrivals *'are in a distressed state.'* Those being deported were, however, overall being replaced with fresh arrivals from Ireland, but the vestry was confident that the majority were healthier than those who arrived earlier in the year, with fewer making claims on the parish and a significant number moving on to other parts of the country. The *Mercury* on 3 September reported that the cost of relieving the Irish poor for the final week of August was £227, this compared with an average weekly cost of about £1500 just a few weeks earlier.

By early autumn, typhus cases were on the decline. There were fewer patients in the sheds and on the lazarettos. Without a patient, in mid-September the *Newcastle* was decommissioned and the following month the *Akbar* was returned to the government.

The town's authorities once again turned to begging and vagrancy. On 18 November, and reported in the *Mercury* the following day, an extraordinary meeting of the Select Vestry, the Health Committee and local magistrates took place in the town. A Vestry member, Mr Poole, complained that there was a great difficulty in:

> *'...attempting to free the town of the great evils under which it presently laboured. In spite of the law there existed in the town a class of people who steadily avoided applying to the parish, being in no doubt well aware that if they did they would be immediately removed.'*

Poole implored the magistrates to use the Vagrancy Act to deal with such people. Borough Magistrate, Edward Rushton, informed the meeting that the full force of the Act was in use and moreover all the town's local jails were full with more than 700 people incarcerated. If one witnessed, said Rushton:

> '... the shivering wretches at the parish office on Fenwick Street looking for relief then prisons for seven thousand would be required.'

Some people, he added, were glad to be sentenced to imprisonment; at least they could get something to eat there. Begging, the meeting determined, was still a huge problem and the police needed to do more to combat it and if those apprehended are Irish, then they should be removed back to their home country.

* *

At the end of the year, Liverpool was left to assess the impact of the arrival of thousands of Irish migrants, as well as the human cost of typhus and other diseases. In his November report, the registrar of Great Howard Street calculated that *'290,000 Irish had, so far, landed in Liverpool'* but not all were famine victims or paupers. A significant majority moved on to other parts of the country or emigrated to America. Despite over 15,000 being returned to Ireland under the *Removal of Paupers Act*, he estimated that about 90,000 remained in Liverpool.

Illness and disease had taken a severe toll; Duncan's 1847 medical report estimated that approximately 100,000 people had contracted typhus, diarrhoea, dysentery, or measles. 7,219 victims who lost their lives were buried in paupers' graves in the cemeteries of St. Mary's and St Martin in the Fields, Oxford Street North (now Silvester Street). Typhus, the biggest killer, caused the deaths of 5,845, more than 80% of whom were Irish Famine immigrants. Duncan calculated that 4,000 children were orphaned that year. He deplored the loss of *'...many comfortable citizens who might have been alive'* had they not encountered the Irish paupers. He included amongst that group the ten Catholic priests, commemorated in a memorial at St. Patrick's Church, Park Road, Toxteth.

Peter Nightingale, St Anthony's who died on 2 March, aged 32
William Parker, St Patrick's, 27 April, aged 43
Thomas Kelly, St Joseph's, 1 May, aged 28
James Francis Appleton, St Peter's, 28 May, aged 40
John Austin Gilbert, St Mary's, 31 May, aged 27
Richard Grayston, St Patrick's, 16 June, aged 33
James Hagger, St Patrick's, 23 June, aged 29
William Vincent Dale, St Mary's, 26 June, aged 48
Robert Gillow, St Nicholas', 22 August, aged 35
John Fielding Whitaker, St Joseph's, 28 September, aged 36

About 20-30 doctors and nurses also fell victim to typhus. The lives of most of the other fatalities are, however relatively unknown. They included dock workers, carpenters, teachers, domestic servants, barbers, parish relieving officers, prisoners and many, many more. In the grounds of St Anthony's Church 2,303 victims were interred during 1847. Some of the names of those buried in the parish cemeteries are unknown, but record keepers at St. Anthony's were able to identify all those laid to rest in its grounds. Many shared the same surname, with whole families amongst those who perished. Containing the names of all those buried on site, in 1997 St Anthony's church, published a special booklet *(The Great Hunger Commemoration Service)* to mark the anniversary of the famine. A sample of surnames and the age ranges of those who perished, exemplifies the devastating impact of the famine and disease.

Brennan; 10 died – ages ranged from 0-80
Burns; 32 died – range 0-80
Connelly; 12 died – range 1-66
Doyle; 11 died – range 1-46
Gallagher; 16 died – range 1-60
Kelly; 22 died – range 1-67
McDonnell : 19 died – range 0-66
McKeon; 11 died – range 1-65
Murphy; 35 died – range 0-80
Quinn; 15 died – range 0-56

As an appropriate soubriquet, Black '47 remains controversial, but, in terms of loss of life, it was a devastating, horrific year for Ireland and its people, the consequence of which also severely impacted on Liverpool. The famine persisted for another four years, eventually claiming over one million lives with a million more escaping overseas to survive. The famine's effects transformed Ireland forever. For the remainder of the nineteenth century, as farming methods evolved and periodical evictions continued, tens of thousands of Irish citizens boarded ships and arrived in Liverpool. They, like their earlier predecessors, helped to change the city forever.

6. Sectarian Town: Rebellious Town

In Liverpool, Sectarianism (an excessive devotion to a particular group or sect) periodically raised its head in the town. The division between Protestants and Catholics was prone to bouts of violence. The animosity can locally be traced to the late eighteenth century with the establishment of the town's first Orange Lodge and the annual parades celebrating William of Orange's 1690 victory at the Battle of the Boyne. In the early decades of the nineteenth century, violent clashes intensified and Orange Lodge parades were banned. In the early 1840s, Liverpool's Protestants pressurised the authorities to reinstate the parades and many of the town's Catholics were prepared to take matters into their own hands at any sign of a Protestant celebratory event.

In the 1840s, sectarian disorder was to seriously alarm the authorities, though they were, arguably, more anxious about the emergence of two separate, but sometimes closely linked organisations agitating for political change. The Chartists, campaigned to change the British political system, arguing for greater parliamentary representation for the working class. Meanwhile, believing that Ireland should no longer be a part of the United Kingdom, the Irish Confederates, agitated for a return to independence. Chartism, though not as popular in Liverpool as in other parts of northern England, did have support in the town; meanwhile, the settled Irish, believing an organised campaign in Liverpool in support of their fellow homeland Irish Confederates, felt that change was imminent.

Sectarian Violence

At the turn of the eighteenth and nineteenth centuries Liverpool was a predominantly Protestant town. in the first early decades of the nineteenth century, with more work available, the town's population expanded, many of whom were Irish Catholics seeking employment. Their arrival increased tension between the two religious groups. The *Liverpool Mercury* on 19 June 1819 predicted conflict between the *'orange and the green'* when its headline read, *'Orange lodge procession planned for July 12 will be attacked by Irish'*. The prediction turned out to be correct. As the procession entered the town centre, the walkers were met by an estimated 2,000 missile throwing Irish. This was to be the first of many clashes in the first half of the nineteenth century.

In 1822, following serious clashes in the town centre, Liverpool council banned the Orange Lodge procession. Rumours of a 12 July 1835 orange procession spread amongst the Irish. Thousands gathered and the day ended with 3,000 Catholics attacking the Vauxhall Road bridewell and barracks. The disturbance required 500 Special Constables and 200 soldiers to calm the situation. Hundreds were arrested, 43 of whom were eventually convicted of violent disorder, each receiving a six-month prison sentence.

Several Tory councillors were members of orange lodges and in 1842, following the election of a Tory led authority, Protestants were confident that the 12 July processions would be reinstated by the council. They believed there was little difference between the unprohibited Catholic custom of celebrating St. Patrick's Day with annual, and their 12 July parade. Thousands of Catholics had indeed paraded from the town centre to St. Anthony's Church on Scotland Road, so the Orange Lodges argued for the same privilege. Although some Tory Councillors firmly believed the procession should be restored, many other councillors felt that restoration was too risky. Chief magistrate, Edward Rushton also agreed that there was a great probability of violence and serious injury and the distinct possibility of someone being killed.

An Irish born Anglican priest, appointed reverend of St Jude's Church, Hardwick Street in 1834, though not a member, was the undisputed religious and political voice of the Orange Order. In 1848, Hugh McNeile was transferred to St Paul's, Prince's Park, a 2,000 plus seat church especially built for him. A fervent anti-Catholic and powerful orator, McNeile became chairman of the Liverpool Protestant Association, the same year. He was a tub-thumping sermoniser who could lecture his congregation, on subjects such as *'No Popery'*, for up to 90 minutes.

His articles and letters regularly appeared in the Liverpool press. Frank Neal (Sectarian *Violence: The Liverpool Experience*, 1819-1914) claims that McNeile believed that *'...the Roman Catholic Church was the enemy of Christianity and the Pope was the Antichrist.'* Adding that McNeile: *'...had difficulty in using the word religion when referring to Roman Catholics,'* McNeile, often credited with helping the Tories to take control of the council, had great support amongst Protestant shipwrights, ships' carpenters and other similar dock workers who lived close to their workplaces in the south dockyards.

In the months leading to 12 July 1842, letters appeared in the newspapers urging Protestants to plan for a procession. Reported in the local press, rumours and reports of well organised orange preparations for 12 July spread throughout the town. An anonymous author wrote to the *Liverpool Journal* on 28 May saying he witnessed:

> *'Orangemen with collector's books going around working class districts collecting money for flags and sashes.'*

The author said he spoke to one Orangeman who told him their aim was *'to drive the Irish out of town'*. The Orangeman said the procession could not be stopped as *'...the mayor had promised the marchers police protection.'*

The under-pressure mayor, John Shaw Leigh, though sympathetic to Protestant demands confirmed the existing ban on orange processions, but went further and banned all future St Patrick's Day parades. Sceptical, the *Journal* believed the orange procession would go ahead, condemning it for being an excuse to *'...insult Irish Catholics.'* On 23 June, the paper reported that a considerable body of Orangemen, met at Toxteth Hall where it was resolved to march through the town.

Rushton, and most other magistrates were unwavering in their belief that the procession should not proceed. On 28 June, magistrates met with Orange Lodge leaders and implored them to cancel the parade.

The Orangemen agreed and returned to their lodges to inform their members. However, many were determined to stick to their plans. Appearing increasingly likely that some sort of procession would proceed, Rushton ordered Head Constable, Michael Whitty, to assemble a body of police officers to quell the expected disturbances.

The *Liverpool Albion* reported that on 11 July, the eve of the procession, flags and buntings were hung from houses in some Protestant homes on the 12th, some 2,000 Orangemen gathered in Toxteth at St. James' Place to prepare for a march. Rushton, Whitty and the mayor spent the day travelling to and from St. James' Place to the town hall observing and reporting on the day's events. Meanwhile a mile or two from Toxteth, thousands of Irish gathered in the north of the town with the intention of preventing the parade going ahead. In the early afternoon, the orange parade commenced its half mile journey to the Phoenix Inn on Mount Pleasant and were met by missiles from some Irish Catholics who had managed to break the police cordons preventing them from confronting marchers.

After spending a few hours drinking, at 8.00 p.m. the Orangemen returned to St. James Place, but this time they were met head on by *'several thousand-stone throwing Irish.'* Whitty ordered a mounted police charge to disperse the Irish, while ordering other officers to arrest offenders. The police eventually managed to quell the disturbances, but the evening's events were not an end to the violence.

The following day there were reports of Irishmen searching for Protestants to attack. In Adlington Street, Vauxhall, two Protestant men were pursued, caught by a mob and violently attacked. The men required treatment at the Northern Hospital. There were further reports of Protestant ships' carpenters wandering the town meting out vengeance upon Irishmen. The violence, which continued on the 14th, tragically conclude on the 15th.

Catherine Carney, a 34-year-old Irishwoman, born in County Donegal, was violently attacked outside St James Church in Toxteth. Badly injured, she was transported to the southern Hospital, where she was able to report the incident to the police. Reported in the *Albion*, Catherine said two men approached her, put their hands on her shoulders and called her an *'Irish bitch'* before running away. A few moments later, she said, they returned, beat her to the ground and kicked her as she lay defenceless. She reported that one of the men shouted, *'We'll finish you, you Irish bitch.'* She was however unable to describe her assailants.

Very weak and seriously ill, upon arrival in hospital, Catherine was unaware that she had also be the victim of a knife attack. In an attempt to solicit further information, the police called on Catherine during her hospital convalescence. Tragically, however, on 5 August, Catherine died of her injuries. The inquest jury returned a verdict of *'wilful murder by persons unknown.'* A victim of sectarian violence, her killers were never apprehended.

Sectarian violence, exacerbated by arrival of Irish migrants during the famine period, remained constant throughout the remainder of the decade, though never matching the disturbances of 1842.

Chartism

'The government are totally indifferent to the wellbeing and welfare of the working classes' so declared Operative Porter, Thomas Jones, at a public meeting of Liverpool Chartists on 16 August 1842. Addressing a gathering of over 200 people in the Chartist Hall, Preston Street (between Dale Street and Victoria Street), Jones maintained that, though the government was squarely on the side of employers, political events were moving in the right direction for working class 'men', they were on the path to parliamentary representation.

Escalating strikes, accompanied by meetings and demonstrations in towns in the north of England such as Warrington, Preston and Leeds, had at times ended in riot. Consequently, dozens of police officers attended any Chartist gathering in northern towns.

Chartism, taking its name from the People's Charter of 1838, was a national protest movement. When established, only 18 per cent of the adult male population of Britain could vote (before 1832 just 10 per cent could vote). Much of the working class, living in poverty, were without a voice in politics. The ultimate goal of the Chartists, as stated in the first minutes of the London Working Men's Association, was:

> '...to seek by every legal means to place all classes of society in possession of their equal, political, and social rights'.

This would be achieved by campaigning for six key changes to the parliamentary system: Universal suffrage (votes for all men); abolition of property qualifications for members of parliament; annual parliamentary elections; equal representation; payment of MPs and a vote by secret ballot.

Using a network of newspapers, as well as mass meetings and speeches, the Chartists message quickly spread. The movement had a huge amount of support from the working classes, particularly in industrialised areas. There was however a split between those who wished to use peaceful *'moral force'* and those who believed in the use of *'physical force'* to achieve the aims of the Charter. Leaders, such as the author of the People's Charter, William Lovett, a moral force Chartist, were opposed by other physical force leaders, such as Feargus O'Connor.

The Chartist campaign for change began peacefully in 1839 with the use of petitions, collected and presented to Parliament, the largest of which was said to have contained almost six million signatures. This was presented to and rejected by Parliament. A second, containing

3.3 million signatures, was again presented in May 1842. On a vote of 287 to 49, it too was rejected by MPs. As the petition was being presented, there were already strikes and disturbances taking place in some parts of the country but, with the latest rejection, unrest spread and intensified.

In the wake of parliament's second rejection, in the summer of 1842 a great wave of strikes engulfed Lancashire and Yorkshire. The strikes began in the Staffordshire coalfields in July when miners demanded a reduction in hours and an increase in pay. The miners also linked their economic demands with political demands when several meetings passed resolutions stating that *'nothing but the People's Charter can give us a fair day's wage for a fair day's work.'*

By August, effecting factories and mills as well as mines, the strikes were widespread with thousands of employees refusing to work. Strikers were active picketing, marching and demonstrating.

Occasionally the events ended in violence between the strikers and the police sent in to break up picket lines, for example. On one such occasion, in Preston on 13 August, four men were shot dead during what became known as the *'Plug Plot'* riots, so called because the strikers took plugs from steam boilers to prevent their operation. There were also disturbances in Yorkshire including at Bradford, Huddersfield and Hunslet; at least six people died in a riot at Halifax. Liverpool, being at the time a port town with a predominantly casual workforce, was not affected by strikes, but there was sympathy for the strikers and for Chartism. Thousands of Liverpool citizens signed the 1839 and 1842 Charters, for example.

After the Preston Street meeting on 13 August 1842 in Liverpool town centre, police heard rumour of Chartists from parts of Lancashire marching to Liverpool with the intention of causing a riot. Chief Constable Whitty was instructed by magistrate, Edward Rushton, to determine the truth of the stories. Whitty rode out to Old Swan, but having spent a few hours there on observation, returned to town and declared the rumours false. That very evening, however, hundreds of Chartists met in the Assembly Rooms, Lord Nelson Street. The returning Whitty, along with Rushton and the Town Clerk and Attorney, William Shuttle worth, were at the meeting in observance. The *Liverpool Journal* of the 20th reported that the *'three men were gravely concerned about the possibility of the law being broken.'* Nothing untoward unfolded, though Whitty did complain that he had his *'pocket picked and a silk handkerchief stolen.'*

The summer strikes concluded with hundreds of people arrested across parts of Lancashire and committed for trial at Liverpool. At the Sessions House, especially reconstructed to accommodate three judges including Chief Justice Lord Abinger, the trials opened on 15 October. The charges and the numbers of defendants were:

Riot 40
Riot and arson 4
Riot and conspiracy 14
Riot and assault 3
Riot and demolition 28
Riot and stealing 18
Sedition 2

The *Journal* on the 20th listed the names and further details of the defendants, including their ages, except for defendant, Joseph Thomas, who was described as *'an idiotic black man.'* Chartist leader Feargus O'Connor was listed to appear in court too, but illness prevented him attending. His trial was postponed to the following

March at Lancaster. The 12-man jury included an MP, Thomas Green and a knight of the realm, Sir Thomas Whitehead. In his opening address, Abinger announced that he believed that all the defendants should be facing charges of High Treason. The strikes, he added, were a Chartist conspiracy and furthermore, although:

> '...the country is suffering an economic downturn its effects are greatly exaggerated... I have not seen the people suffering from high prices or loss of labour.'

The *Journal* responded by asking a direct question: *'How would he know?'*

Most defendants were found guilty; their sentences ranged from three months to two and a half years' imprisonment with hard labour, to be served at Kirkdale. The youngest defendant, Jane Garvey, aged eleven, was found guilty of riot, but spared jail because of her age. The youngest male, George Turner, aged twelve, was also found guilty of riot; he was, however, sentenced to nine months' imprisonment.

The Lancaster trial of O'Connor and 57 others (including almost all the Chartist national executive) failed: none were convicted on the serious charges of sedition and conspiracy, and those found guilty of minor offences were never actually sentenced. Chartism went into something of a lull in the mid 1840s, though O'Connor did visit Liverpool on a couple of occasions to address Chartists meetings including a gathering of hundreds at the Assembly Rooms, in July 1844.

In 1848, revolutions swept many parts of Europe, and Chartists' confidence was once more revived. In April, the third and final

Chartist petition was presented to Parliament. A mass meeting on Kennington Common in South London was organised to accompany its presentation, but the fearful government deployed the military. There was no disturbance, despite yet another government rejection. The Chartist never immediately lost hope. On Sunday 11 June 1848 hundreds of Chartists gathered on the north shore at Bootle to listen to local Chartist leaders. Thomas Jones, still a leading spokesman, called for a *'speedy enactment of the Charter.'* He added that it was a necessity to aid the working class to promote the:

> *'...amelioration of their physical condition.'* The middle class, he went on, *'...are the enemy of the people... they steal half the produce of the people.'*

The *Liverpool Mercury*, reporting the meeting in its edition on the 14th, reminded readers of the recent arrest and trials of Chartists in London and warned the Liverpool Chartists that *'...if they continue their agitation, they face transportation.'* There was a further Chartist meeting on 28 June at the Music Hall in Bold Street with several speakers repeating the demands of Jones at Bootle.

1848, however, was the last hurrah of Chartism as the movement went into decline nationally and locally. The strikes and demonstrations dissipated, no further petitions were presented to Parliament and working class political rights would have to wait several more years.

Irish Rebels

The Chartists at the local 1848 gatherings shared platforms with Irish Confederates. The Irish Confederation was an Irish nationalist independence group established by individuals who had seceded from the Irish Repeal Association. Led by Daniel O'Connell, the latter association campaigned for a repeal of the 1800 Act of Union of which made Ireland a part of the UK. Repeal of the act appeared increasingly unlikely which frustrated many Irish nationalists who decided to form a separate organisation to put pressure on the British government. In January 1847, the Irish Confederation was formed. In Liverpool, with its substantial Irish born population, support for the Confederation was considerable. Though never openly declaring the use of rebellion, many of its members and supporters believed it the most likely method to achieve their goal of an independent Ireland, particularly as the country was during the devastating famine.

A leading member of the Confederation in Liverpool was Doctor Lawrence Reynolds. Sharing the platform with the Chartists at the June 1848 Bootle meeting, Reynolds proclaimed that in order to ensure Ireland's freedom, members would need to form private clubs and not meet in public. His words reported in the *Mercury*, Reynolds declared:

> *'Every street in Liverpool should have its club, every village its club. Every officer of those clubs should have a rifle, every committee man a musket and every member should have his pike.'*

This clear public statement certainly alarmed the authorities. Edward Rushton had earlier in the year written to the Home Secretary informing him that Head Constable Dowling had instigated surveillance measures against the Chartists; the Confederates would now also be closely watched.

Fearing an Irish rebellion, the Liverpool police force adopted covert and overt methods to destabilise and weaken the Confederates and to disrupt any possible plans for rebellion. The final total is uncertain, but estimates suggest that around 30 to 40 Confederate Clubs, averaging 100-200 members, were established across the town. Covertly, the authorities required police spies and informers to gather information on the inner workings and plans of the clubs. In early July, Dowling, warning of the dangers of the Confederates, wrote to the mayor to explain his plan of infiltration:

> 'There are a few men to be relied upon to run the risk of giving information and fewer still upon whom dependence could be placed. Those from whom I obtain particulars at present live in a constant state of alarm fearing that the least discovery would consign them to death. If it were merely required that each person joining these clubs should enrol himself and so become a member, without the ceremony of others introducing and vouching for him, there would be not the least difficulty of acquiring of every word or movement going on.'

Dowling stressed that the infiltrators had to be Irish and hinted that it would be preferable if they too were Catholic. Overtly, the authorities publicly displayed its strength across the town. For example:

- Hundreds of policemen were trained in the use of muskets
- 2,000 troops, were drafted in from Manchester and Blackburn and based in a military camp in Breck Road, Everton
- Thousands of additional special constables were sworn in following meetings in   every ward in the town

On Saturday 29 July, moreover, there was an attempt to enlist 500 hundred dockers as special constables; they all immediately refused and were dismissed from their jobs. A few dozen of the men returned to the docks the following Monday, signed up as special constables and were reinstated.

The methods quickly brought results. Reynolds, owner of an ironmonger's shop on Vauxhall Road, his employees and associates were being watched and followed. In mid July two of Reynolds' temporary employees, Henry Banner and Joseph Cuddy, were spotted carrying sacks and stopped by police. The sacks contained pikes. The men were charged with possession of weapons and on 24 July appeared at the magistrate's court. Banner and Cuddy admitted possession, but said the pikes were not intended for Confederate Clubs but for transportation to Manchester.

Police officer, Hall, who detained the men, told the court that he had spoken to Cuddy on an earlier occasion and the defendant had informed him that he was a salesman for Dr Reynolds, a dealer of bayonets, cutlasses, swords and pikes. Cuddy, said Hall, had delivered weapons to several Confederate Clubs. In his defence, Cuddy said that Reynolds' ironmongery was not a secret location as much of his produce was on display in the shop window. The two men were found guilty and fined.

Also in July, the police raided the home of a tailor and Confederate Club member, Patrick Murphy, and discovered a *'minute book,'* which detailed suggestions on how to create and organise clubs under the command of captains and superintendents. The minute book also referred to Reynolds using his ironmonger's business as a front to arm the Confederates.

The minute book provided the necessary evidence to clamp down on the Liverpool Confederates. A warrant was issued for the arrest of Reynolds. His shop and home were raided, but the doctor had disappeared. Meanwhile, Dowling's plan to infiltrate Confederate meetings was bearing fruition. The infiltrators (or police spies) had gathered enough information to arrest and charge leading Confederates with conspiracy at least.

At the December assizes, ten Confederates were charged with:

> *'Conspiracy to excite tumult and insurrection'* and *'Sending arms to Ireland for the purpose of insurrection and to create insurrection in England.'*

The defendants were:

> Francis O'Donnell; 29, Gentleman of Education
> Edward Murphy; 20, Tailor
> Peter Delamere; 32, Clerk
> Joseph Cuddy; 32, Salesman
> Robert Hopper; 22, Joiner
> Mathew Somers; 23, Provisions Dealer
> Martin Boshell; 22, Clerk
> James O'Brien; 22, Labourer
> George Smythe; 23, Hatter
> TB McManus; no age, Shipping Agent

Deeming the charges so serious, the government's case was led by the Attorney General, Sir John Jervis, a driving force behind the *Treason Felony Act* enacted in 1848 to especially prosecute Chartists and Confederates. In his opening address, he said the men in the dock:

'...had conspired to form a league with the Chartists.' They intended, to create a diversion by engaging in a rising in Liverpool so as to aid rebellion in Ireland.'

Furthermore, the minute book provided clear evidence of the men's guilt. Jervis had at his command a whole host of prosecution witnesses.

Newspaper reporter Simon Harker told the court that he attended several Confederate and Chartist public meetings. In one at the Music Hall, Bold Street, he heard Mathew Somers inform his audience that they could obtain pikes from Dr Reynolds that very evening if they so wished.

A second witness, police officer and infiltrator, Peter McAnally, said he attended a Confederate meeting in a house in Circus Street (near William Brown Street) at which several of the defendants were present. He claimed that members were informed that *'many clubs were armed and ready to go.'*

More than ten further witnesses gave evidence for the prosecution including some neighbours of the defendants, one of whom told the court that he had been asked *'to join a club and take up arms.'*

Defending barristers attacked the police spies and reporters. The spies, they claimed, were clearly unable to make notes at the meetings, as doing so would have attracted suspicion, therefore their memories of who said what to whom could not be relied upon.

Officer McAnally did not produce written notes. Furthermore, reporters such as Harker were approached by the police months after the meetings they attended. Harker never reported the words he gave in evidence, so how could he now be trusted. The defendants working for Reynolds, never made secret their employment. The shop was known to sell all manner of possible weaponry, so how could the men be accused of conspiracy?

As for the allegation of a conspiracy between Chartists and Confederates, where were the Chartists? One defending barrister claimed that Reynolds used the Confederates to try to sell them weapons and line his own pockets. The court heard that the police believed that Reynolds had boarded a Liverpool ship and escaped to New York.

Despite defence pleas, all defendants, bar Delamere, were found guilty. McManus was sentenced to transportation with the other eight men facing sentences ranging from six months to two years.

If there ever was a serious chance of a rebellion in Liverpool in 1848, and historians disagree over its realisation, it concluded with the December trial. Meanwhile, Reynolds remains something of a mystery figure. Why did he openly declare at public meetings his belief in the establishment of Confederate Clubs with the purpose of rebellion, yet he was one of the few leaders not to be apprehended and convicted?

Finally, any threat of rebellion in Ireland had been crushed earlier that year with the conviction of Confederate leaders including William O'Brien and John Mitchell who were both sentenced to transportation, which ended any chance of a planned uprising anywhere in the UK. If rebellion could not occur in Ireland, it was unlikely to begin in Liverpool.

Epilogue

The abolition of the slave trade in 1807 did not herald the demise of Liverpool as some of the prophets of doom had forecast at the time. In the first few decades of the nineteenth century Liverpool's industry and population grew steadily, but it was 1840s which proved to be the catalyst for rapid and dramatic change. In terms of industry and work, the development of the port and the increase in shipping drove change. Tens of thousands were employed on the docks as the quay space almost doubled. As the century progressed Liverpool went on to become one of the world's most important ports with tens of thousands of tons of goods imported and exported annually.

Prior to 1840, though beginning to grow, the emigrant trade was still a minor component of the port's overall business. By the end of the decade, however, with the rapid development of steam shipping, it became fundamental to growth. Arriving from all over Europe, by 1930, an unbelievable 13 million emigrants were to pass through Liverpool the port on to new lives in America, Australia and other far off countries.

In the long run, emigration and the international shipping trade changed the demographics of the town. Usually out of financial necessity, many thousands of the European emigrants, intending to board a ship in Liverpool to move on, found work and remained in the town. From the 1860s, demographics changed again, as many hundreds of Asian and African seamen, from countries such as China and India, arrived and decided to stay in Liverpool.

The greatest demographic change was however brought about in the mid to late-nineteenth century by the Irish. Analysis of the pre-famine census reveals that Irish-born people accounted for over 17 per cent of the population in Liverpool, about 41,000. By 1851 this figure had officially risen to over 22 per cent, almost 84,000. This is probably an underestimation as many Irish emigrants arriving during the famine hid themselves away to avoid the census, under fear of deportation.

Mostly Catholics, the famine Irish changed the religious and political dynamic of the town. Dozens of Catholic churches were built, whilst in 1885 the parliamentary constituency of Scotland (named after Scotland Road) was the only constituency outside the island of Ireland to return an Irish Nationalist Party MP, TP O'Connor. The late nineteenth and early twentieth century did not though see a diminution in sectarian violence, which fluctuated in intensity over the next century or so.

As they were before and during the 1840s, Liverpool's prosperous citizens continued to amass riches and they helped changed the physical outlook of the town particularly around the Lime Street area. Some wished to display their wealth to the world and one way to demonstrate this was in grand public buildings. Successful businessmen, for example, bought shares in the neo-classical St. George's Hall, construction of which began in 1841; the building opened in 1854.

The following year work began on William Brown Library, named after the MP, banker and merchant, whose statue stands in St. George's Hall, who funded the building. Similarly designed, to St. George's, the building opened to the public in 1860. Other neo-classical building opened on William Brown Street shortly afterwards. Although Liverpool Zoo closed in 1867, many places of entertainment, such as the Philharmonic Hall, continued to thrive. On the sporting front, the Grand National has gone on to become *'the world's most famous horserace'*.

With respect to crime and punishment, public hanging, like transportation, was removed from the statute books in 1868. It was not, however, until the *Infanticide Act* of 1922 that the killing of a newborn baby by its mother was no longer considered a capital crime and factors such as the mental state of the mother could be used in the woman's defence. Liverpool Borough Jail on Great Howard Street was closed in 1855 to be replaced by the newly opened Walton Prison. Kirkdale Prison, considered at the time one of the unhealthiest institutions of its kind in Europe, was closed in 1897.

The economic divide continued, with poverty remaining deep and ingrained in much of Liverpool's population. The plan to clear the town of court housing was never completed. Indeed, there were still families living in such accommodation more than one hundred years after Doctor Duncan's recommendation to demolish the worst of it.

Liverpool workhouse was always near capacity until its closure in 1923. The night asylums remained open for a couple of more decades, whilst casualism on the docks persisted well into the twentieth century. The rebellious element for which Liverpool is often renowned re-emerged in the twentieth century with disputes over wages and conditions by transport workers in 1911 and the police in 1919, for example.

By the end of the 1840s, despite improvements in health indicated by the average age of death which rose from 17 in 1841 to 26 in 1851, tragedies reoccurred as killer diseases returned. Liverpool, for example, suffered further epidemics of cholera in 1854 and 1866. Campaigns to improve health were ceaseless.